Angels in My Classroom

Angels in My Classroom

How Second Graders Saved My Life

By: Lee-Ann Meredith

Lee-Ann Meredith Publishing

This book is dedicated to my son and daughter. I am so proud of the fine man and woman you have grown to be. You are truly the lights of my life.

If you light a lamp for someone else, it will also brighten your path.

—Buddha

The Educator's Room, LLC
P.O. Box 311770, Atlanta, GA 31131
Printed in the United States of America

ISBN 13-:978-0692250259

Back and front cover designed by: Frank DeJohns

I would like to acknowledge the following angels who have helped me through my journey. My gratitude is overwhelming.

To every student and parent in my classroom, you were truly my teachers.

To the teachers, administrators, and all the staff who worked with me at my wonderful school, you gave me momentum, made me laugh, and kept me on my toes.

To my kids, I am delighted we made it through all the stuff, and came out of it as people who enjoy each other's company. I love both of you and your families. You are my most precious gifts.

To Lourdes Guerrero (my Sue), Pat Reynolds, and Owen and Lena Reynolds, my building and loan partners, you were my rocks during the darkest days. Your support and friendship is more beautiful than I can ever express in words.

To Karen, who walked a similar path and nudged me along the way. I believe in this life and many others, you have been my student, teacher, and friend.

To Marva, Robin, and PD, you have been my balm and my truest friends.

To my sisters and brother, and their families, we are an awesome team and you are the best laugh-creators I've ever met.

To Frank DeJohns, your art, laughter, and friendship have been a delight. Watching your growth into a truly remarkable teacher has been one of my richest rewards.

To Jenny F. and Frank S., you were my therapists. You took care of my body and soul through the dark and lonely days, and helped me keep perspective on my world.

To Fran Warren, for your support and belief in this book. Your gifts to educators are beyond measure.

To all those crazy friends of my children, who kept me young, ate my food, and still come back to give me hugs. You give me hope for the future.

I am rich in friends and I believe each one of you helped me on this sometimes difficult and sometime joyous path. You are too numerous to name. To that, I say, aren't I blessed? Thank you all!

CONTENTS

NOTE: Each child in this story is a composite of many children. No actual

name of any student in Room 203 is used.

INTRODUCTION

MY ANGELS

Seven-year-old Arthur used to sneak up behind me and utter in this crazy *sotto voce*, "You're beautiful!" Then he ran away and hid behind his desk. He would also sometimes whisper in that same voice, "I hate you!" I always laughed when he said that because I knew it wasn't true.

I've taught a few hundred second graders in 13 years and I formed a connection with every one of them. Each one was a spark, a teacher who taught the teacher. Each one was a wish. More than anything, they were my angels.

I was called to teaching. It took me years to realize it and follow the call. I think my soul knew the right time and the right place. This is the story of my journey of more than a dozen years

teaching in the same school, same room, and same grade. I

taught them reading, math, science, and everything else I could.

In return, they saved me when my world caved in.

Margaret was a student in my very difficult class the year

my husband, Mark, died. Her little sister had died after a long

illness when Margaret was in kindergarten. She was having a hard

time coping with the loss. When my husband was entering

hospice, another girl asked me if Mr. Meredith was going to get

better. Little feisty Margaret stepped between the other child

and me. In a very mature voice, her eyes opened wide, she told

her classmate, "We are hoping for the best."

Ten years later, it still brings tears to my eyes. My loss

brought her healing that year because she wanted to protect me.

When my life was more than I could bear—during Mark's

battle with cancer, my son's immense grief, and my daughter's

struggle with loss, distrust, and just plain old ADHD—the angels in my room distracted me. They gave me love. They made me laugh. They lifted my soul with a purpose for being.

Mark was diagnosed with colon cancer during my first year in the classroom. I had been a bookkeeper and accountant part-time for years. I was following the call, a wild passion to teach. I was teaching at a Chicago public school on the northwest side of the city. It was the same school my own children attended. I was in the grade I wanted. My teaching dreams had come true.

My personal life was a mixed bag of contentment and chaos. I felt I needed to be the bedrock for my family. My lovely husband encouraged me to teach. He listened and laughed at the stories I told of my days. He endured chemotherapy, radiation, and several surgeries with amazing fortitude and humor. He told jokes about losing his hair, saying, "Fuzzy Wuzzy wasn't fuzzy, was he?" He baked cookies for sick friends with no regard to the tremendous amount of pain he was in. He was bound and determined to enjoy the rest of his life.

We were able to maintain a semblance of a normally functioning home life. Our kids were in their early teens, a difficult age by any measure. My son was heartbroken and angry at his dad's illness. My daughter was constantly positive, to the point of denial. Mark and I joked we lived with Mr. Doom and Gloom and Pollyanna.

I kept hoping we could beat the cancer, that it would all become a terrible dream, a hurdle we had jumped over. I felt if I had any doubt in Mark's ability to win the battle, he would certainly die. I was steadfastly optimistic.

The surgeon who performed Mark's liver resection told me he had bought Mark a couple of years, but he hadn't cured him. I never told anyone. Only my mom and my minister heard the doctor state it. I locked it in my heart and hoped it would turn out to be a mistake. I didn't tell him until Mark was in hospice a-year-and-a-half later.

Mark died on February 13, 2003. My class was sad for me but—think like a second grader—the Valentine's Day party was the next day. This group was so tough that only one old retired

teacher would sub for more than two days at a time. They

chewed up those subs and spit them out.

The substitute on the day of Mark's death had everyone

write sympathy cards. They copied them from the board and

decorated them with pink and purple hearts. Unfortunately, the

substitute spelled like a second grader.

Dear Ms. Meredith,

We are sorry that Mr. Meredith past.

Happy Valentine's Day!

How could I not laugh? They loved me even when I was a

grouchy, sad old thing. How beautiful is that?

Yes, they were my angels, and this is the story of how they

saved me.

CHAPTER 1

AVOIDING TRAIN WRECKS

"My best friend in Nalabama is a grasshopper!"

Flipping her hair, Renée glared at her classmates, daring them to laugh. "And my dad's best friend is a bat." Heads bent down, lips pressed firmly together or hands slapped over their mouths. Eyes rolled, flashed, or squeezed shut. Not one single solitary giggle escaped.

One day I had brought this beautiful orange for my lunch. It was on my table as the kids came in the room that morning. I could smell it across the room. Renée didn't come to the rug with the rest of the class for morning meeting. I had seen her come in, so I asked, "Where's Renée?"

"She's in the closet under the coats. She's eating an orange, Ms. Meredith."

I glanced at my desk. Sure enough, no orange.

"Renée, come here." She climbed out of a pile of coats, scattering hats, scarves, and the contents of backpacks as she emerged. Her face was smeared with orange pulp. She held a half-eaten orange in her hand. I was incredulous. "You're eating my orange."

"This dirty old thing? My daddy gave it to me."

"No, Renée, it's my orange. Throw it away." I sighed.

She stomped across the room to the large metal wastebasket in the front of the room. *Thunk!* She turned around, stomped to her desk, and sat down.

"Come join us on the rug, please."

"*Fine!*"

Later that morning, I smelled orange again. I knew where to look. There was Renée, bent over her desk eating the orange. She hadn't thrown it away. She had just kicked the trashcan. I picked up the can and carried it to her desk. "Throw it away! Now!"

"*Fine!* I hate you!'

I told this story each year to demonstrate what a lack of self-control looks like. My subsequent classes were always stunned and amazed by the audacity of this girl. Her classmates just knew she was who she was. For the most part, they tolerated her. They tried to help her, even when she stole from them. They tried to remind her how to behave.

As with most second-grade classes, the group I had that year had varied personalities and abilities. Three boys in this class were brilliant, among the smartest students I had ever taught. One was a Tolkien elf with his feet on the ground. Paval, another of the boy wonders, was a live wire, zipping around the room all day. The third boy was my unhappy genius, which was never a positive sign.

Another wickedly funny boy, Robin, jumped off the bus on a field trip and ran into traffic. He had super ADHD. His mom had medication for him but said it made him suicidal, as if running into Chicago traffic wasn't. I refused to take him on any more trips unless his mom came along. She tried to persuade me to

take him by beginning to give him his Adderall.

Then there was Medusa. Her beautiful waist-length, black

mane hung in two perfect braids down her back to her waist

when she was calm. But about 75 percent of the time, she wasn't.

She tore at that hair until it stood out like hundreds of snakes. At

least you could tell which mood she was in as she approached the

room.

There was a whole cast of other characters. Renée was

perhaps the highlight of all my years of teaching. She was a little

blue-eyed brunette, a cute girl who was very troubled. She stole.

She tripped people. Her best friend was a grasshopper. Renée

would randomly declare, "Do not take the Lord thy God's name in

dominion," causing me to shake my head and wonder if I had

heard her correctly. She tended to proselytize in the classroom,

attempting to convert my Jewish and Muslim students to her

somewhat skewed version of Christianity. Whenever this

happened, my unhappy genius would lean his face with his finger-smeared glasses and self-cut hair into Renée's face. "I don't believe in God," he'd growl. At this point, the Elf would slink over to me and stage whisper, "Religion alert!"

Medusa would always get worked up when Renée was near. She would flap her arms and shuffle like a crab to get away. The challenge was to separate them before Medusa began to get frustrated. Fortunately for me, the snakes in Medusa's hair seemed to hiss that Renée was coming, and Medusa would skitter away.

One day, when Renée was barking and panting like a puppy, Robin shouted, "Renée! You are not a dog and you're never going to be one!" Renée looked shocked and disappointed. I shut my eyes and took several long deep breaths, willing myself not to laugh at the absurdity of her dramatic flair.

When she complained no one liked her, the rest of the class said things like, "You're wrong. You're our friend." They learned to work around her barks, her staring, and her constant pleas for attention.

When they say it takes a village to raise a child, they know what they're talking about. Parents, grandparents, neighbors, teachers, shopkeepers, doctors—they all influence the people we grow to become.

A classroom that allows kids to grow and learn is a village also. There are the loose general rules you write together. There are the places to keep things, like desks and backpacks. There are friends and an occasional nemesis. Leaders spring from the group. There are people you know you can count on and oddballs who have their charms. We share meals together every day. We each have our jobs to do and our tasks to complete. We work and play together.

We built a village that year. We laughed every day. Usually, someone cried. We listened to each other's ideas. We expanded our knowledge. Our understanding and patience grew. We learned to be tolerant of our differences. Renée's personality, however, was a difficulty that we never completely mastered. It was as if we were a train that had one wheel that was a different size than the rest. We rotated the surrounding wheels so not to put undue stress on them, but if we forgot, the train was off the track.

But I had to keep the hardest part of Renée's story a secret. She was having several petit mal seizures a day. Petit mal seizures last only a few seconds and in Renee's case, she seemed to just stop in her tracks and stare. They also seemed to almost hit an imaginary reset button with her, causing her to forget what she was doing. She was prone to staring at people when she was being annoying also so you never knew when her stare was due to a seizure or stubbornness. She was two years behind the class academically and her mother refused to come to meetings to get her help. She didn't explain her illness to Renée. Instead, Renée thought she was dying because her mother started sleeping with her after Renée's diagnosis. I tried to reassure this scared seven-year-old to no avail.

Since her mom refused to tell Renée what was happening medically, I couldn't address it with the class. This was the dysfunction of our village that year. It was keeping a secret that would have been better told. It would have helped Renée and her classmates survive the ups and downs of village life. It would have added struts to the train wheels and cushioned the biggest bumps.

I fought for Renée. Her mother finally came to a few meetings to get Renée assessed. Things move very slowly when it comes to getting extra help for a child, especially if the parents are not on board. By the end of the year, Renée had been given a learning disability diagnosis. She was getting help with reading and math. She was seeing a social worker for a few minutes biweekly. I was able to get Renée the most help available, but in Chicago public schools that is still limited. I suspected, with her mother's denial and the magnitude of her learning problems, it was too little, too late.

Fast-forward two years. In my class that year, a girl named Rhonda had several medical issues that affected her both physically and academically. She was terribly spoiled at home, which was giving her another disability: the "center of the universe" affliction. The kids who had been with her in kindergarten and first grade knew how she was. But now that she was in second grade, there was a new group of kids in class with her for the first time. They simply did not know what to make of her.

I asked her mom if I could explain to the class about Rhonda's illnesses. The mom readily agreed. I called a class meeting. Rhonda was thrilled!

"You all know Rhonda's arm is different than yours and she walks differently, too," I told them. "Rhonda and I are about to tell you why. First, a baby takes about 40 weeks to grow in a mom to be a healthy baby. Rhonda was born after only 28 weeks. It made her a very sick baby. This has made her family spoil her a little. Isn't that true, Rhonda?"

Rhonda nodded with a self-satisfied smile.

"She also had too much fluid in her brain," I continued. "She has to take a lot of medicine. Sometimes it makes her feel sick, so she gets grumpy. When she's being moody, it's probably the medicine making her that way. She has had more than 15 operations so far. Who's had an operation?"

A few hands rose. Some had their tonsils taken out or an appendix removed. In their 7-year-old minds, stitches and broken bones were operations, too.

Rhonda told the class how she had a tube from her brain to her stomach so the fluid in her head would drain. One of the macho boys shot his hand into the air. "Wait! How did they get a tube in your brain?"

"They used a saw," Rhonda replied. The thought bubbles floated out of their heads and exploded everywhere. Images of handsaws, saber saws, chain saws, and circular saws drifted around the room. Shocked faces spread across the carpet.

"It was a very little saw," I tried to explain. It didn't matter.

The response to this meeting was immediate. The children helped her open her milk or start her coat zipper. She was invited to play tag or jump rope. They saw her as immeasurably brave.

However, she was still spoiled and bossy. If the other kids were tired of her, it was because she was bossing them around, not because of her physical differences. Rhonda could have derailed the class. Instead, we were a village (if you allow me to mix metaphors) that mostly ran on track that year, even if there were a few bumps.

There was the day when I told Rhonda to get to work. She put her hands on her hips and got snippy. "Don't you dare talk to me in that tone of voice!" she growled. Poor Rhonda. I probably shouldn't have laughed but it caught me off guard. It wasn't her best day but it turned out her medication was being adjusted and she was off kilter.

So, yes, a classroom is a village. Every minute won't be

perfect. When we are honest in how we work together, however,

it leads to some wonderful laughter and fun-filled moment.

CHAPTER 2

THE CLASSROOM OF HOPE

"You're lucky to have me as a student because I'm smart."

A beautiful little round-faced Latina with no front teeth, Jonita grinned as she spoke and shook her long black braids as she bobbed her head with pride. It was an unbearably hot August day, and I was walking with her to the air-conditioned computer lab to give her an assessment a few days before the school year began. She reached over and took my hand. We had only met seconds before.

The new second graders came in to be tested one at a time. It was not a hard test for most. They read a story for one minute, explained a list of vocabulary words, and then read a list of 20 sight words. It helped me know where to start them academically. It also gave the two of us a chance to start building our relationship.

Sometimes I was already familiar with a child, for example, if they might have been a younger sibling of a former pupil. Those students greeted me with a big hug. Or it might have been a child from first grade who I "met" several times in the hall when they were doing something they shouldn't have. "Be careful," I'd tell them. "I might be your future."

Some children came in confidently like my darling Jonita. Some were so shy they whispered the answers. Some didn't want to take the test. They just wanted to discuss *Star Wars.* "I bet you don't know Boba Fett isn't human," a brilliant boy named Duncan challenged.

Ha!

"No, he's a Mandalorian bounty hunter," I replied. (One of my first dates with Mark was to see *The Empire Strikes Back*. I was also the mother of a *Star Wars* freak who threw facts at me with lightning speed when he was a tween.) I sighed inwardly. *Here we go again*, I would think to myself. It's either *Star Wars* or Harry Potter with the truly brilliant.

What Duncan saw was a teacher who might understand him.

Each fall, the school halls are full of hope. Each child hopes for the best teacher, friends to play with, and a fun year. Each parent hopes this will be a great year for his or her child. They want a teacher who connects with both parent and child. They're hoping their son or daughter will make huge strides forward. They are counting on no problems in school. No phone calls home. No red pen notes from Ms. Meredith in the agenda.

For teachers, it is a myriad of desires. The dream class sits quietly and works hard. They follow instructions. I hoped to be able to make every single child gain two years of learning squeezed into ten months. Parents would always cooperate. I knew this was called a dream class for a reason. It rarely came true but it was something to which I could aspire.

To me, teaching has always been a calling. Not a career. Not something to do because I couldn't do anything else. Not a job with summers off.

I am hardly a perfect teacher! I have moments I think of that make me cringe. I have said things that I wish I could take back. I have had abysmal failures in my lessons. However, I strived to be better. I always apologized for my temper. I promised I would try not to hurl a marker across the room again. I hated when I did that but, boy, it always got results and it felt so powerful. It was just the wrong kind of results. Instead, I counted slowly, sometimes out loud and sometimes silently with my eyes shut. Or I made a joke. Or I just called out to the universe, *If these guys have guardian angels, it might be the right time for them to flit down and help the kids out a bit.* Or I'd talk to the wall. Any of these magic tricks worked just as well as throwing a marker, and the class responded much more positively.

Let me paint a picture of one evening. It was Open House. Twilight had turned the sky indigo and the overhead lights were on. The classroom was neat and tidy (mostly because I hid a bunch of crap in a bin earlier that evening). It was the second or third week of school.

The classroom was large with high ceilings and tall windows. The desks were pushed into tables for four to six students. There was a large rug in the back of the room with an easel and a rocking chair next to it. The classroom library consisted of five low bookshelves with dozens of tubs filled with books. There were literally over a thousand books waiting to be read. The bins were labeled "space," "dinosaurs," "realistic fiction," or "pigs." The back wall had a bank of cabinets and shelves. Some of the cabinets had vocabulary words listed on them: coincidence, greedy, bitter, bunch. A coat closet opened on the wall opposite the windows. There were numbers above each hook.

About a dozen families—moms, dads, grandparents, and kids—came in the room. They stopped in for a while then left, maybe to visit to a sibling's class or go home to dinner. Other parents would show up later. Frequently, former students' families peeked in and waved.

I tried to shake everyone's hand as they came in. I had known some of the parents for years. Some were new faces and they introduced themselves to me. A few more families wandered in as I talked. If the parents came with the student, the child proudly showed them around the class after they gave me a big hug. Children's voices buzzed.

"I sit here."

"See our pictures on the calendar. I'm number 20."

"This is the library. I like the books about dragons."

I sat on a stool in the front of the room. It was painted yellow with flowers drawn on the legs and a sign taped on one leg that let people know it was the "thinking chair."

Hi! I'm Lee-Ann Meredith, but I guess you know that. I've been here for, let me see, my son is 25 so I guess 20 years. I was here first as a parent. I did the PTA president thing.

I remembered when a friend had asked me if I had considered a nearby neighborhood school for kindergarten for Tom. I went to meet Mr. Z, the principal. The school walls exuded a love for kids. He had this crazy, Brillo hair and always wore double knit pants and wingtip shoes. I recognized a principal who cared about his students. He recognized the "V" for volunteer emblazoned on my forehead. I knew I wanted my kids to go to this school.

When my daughter was in third grade and my son in fifth, I returned to school and got my teaching certificate. This is my 13th year in second grade, teaching in this room. My bachelor's degree is in finance, and I also have enough hours in economics for that to have been my major also. That makes me a math person. Does that surprise you? It does me.

The parents sat and stared at me. I had been hoping for at least a chuckle. They had squeezed into the second-grade chairs. Children played noisily on the rug at the back of the room.

I feel grateful to teach at this school. We have many great things to brag about. We are a Responsive Classroom school. That means we believe that a social curriculum is as important as the academic one. It means kids feel safe to take risks, to be able to make a mistake and still feel secure. We write our own rules as a class. They are—every year—basically these three rules: Treat people the way you want to be treated, be safe, and take care of our room and our school. One of the other teachers always adds: Be the best you can be. I liked the idea so I added it.

I pointed to the rules hanging on the bulletin board in the front of the room. Everyone, even the noisy kids in the back of the room, looked up at them. The kids considered them seriously and nodded their heads. They had written them. The rules belonged to them. They would try to follow them. It was still only September.

I love second graders. They are eager and excited learners. I can't teach them fast enough. They are fact magnets. The brain makes a huge cognitive jump at around age seven. Before that, kids relate everything to themselves and they're very concrete thinkers. Now they can see a much bigger picture. They can begin to grasp how immense space is when we study the solar system or imagine how big a whale is.

Parents sat pondering this. Their heads tilted. Some turned and looked at their daughters and sons.

They are worriers. Remember rubbing a hole in your paper with an eraser when you were a kid? You were probably in second grade. They want to be able to produce things as perfect as what they see in books. They don't understand that the people who produce these things are 30 years older than themselves. They want to be perfect and are frustrated they are not.

Several years ago, the other second-grade teachers and I wrote our own curriculum. We don't use a basal reader. We took the areas they need to learn in science and social studies and selected trade books to teach those concepts. We use these to teach reading

comprehension as well as support the other areas. A few years ago,

we got a new science curriculum that is very hands on. I rewrote the

curriculum to align with it.

I passed out a paper with the first semester goals on it.

Parents looked at it. Some studied it. Others put it in a stack with

all the other stuff they had been given that night.

We start slowly. I call this time of year "tai chi second

grade." At the beginning of the year, we spend a lot of time learning

classroom routines and procedures. We will spend time getting to

know our classmates. By taking time now, the children will learn

how to be independent in their classroom tasks.

This semester, we study emotions and character traits, air

and weather, national symbols, immigration, and whales. After

break, we begin a balance and motion unit and study the circus

while we do that.

The week before winter break, we study New Year's

celebrations around the world. On that Friday, we hold a New

Year's Eve party. 2:00 is midnight. Both second grades go into the hall to count down. We yell Happy New Year and hug and shake noisemakers while trying to eat 12 grapes as quickly as we can.

The Latin families, the majority of the parents, recognized their traditions are being taught. They smiled at me.

I asked for questions. Each year parents asked about spelling. They wanted to know when their child would be expected to spell things correctly when they are writing.

First, I want them to write their ideas down. By third grade, the standardized test requires three written paragraphs. So we need to get ideas down on paper, first and foremost. As the year goes on, the students will get their own five spelling words weekly. These are things they've misspelled during the week. Also, I have spelling groups based on their needs. They will learn they are accountable for their spelling.

The night sped onward. I talked about math and the difficult concepts we would cover. I talked about parents as learning partners with the teacher. I talked about how I never get tired of seven-year-olds. I would then introduce our wonderful

student teacher, if she or he was there.   Frequently, a parent

expressed concern about their individual child and we set up an

appointment or arranged a phone call to discuss it when

everything would be more private and less chaotic.

It was a fun and exhausting evening and I was talked out

by the end of it. I loved watching the kids show off their room. It

was *their* room. I was a pretty important person in it, but it had to

belong to them for the best learning to take place.

As I locked the door at 8 p.m., I thought about the fun,

excitement, and hard work that I was hoping the year would

bring. I was usually hoarse and too pooped after a long, long day

of teaching with an Open House "performance" at the end. Each

year I was filled with hope and wondered what surprises that

group of kids will have in store for me.

CHAPTER 3

BEER PONG AND RELEVANCY

One January, we were studying weight and balance. The students were in pairs or trios with a balance scale. It was a simple contraption: a dowel rod base and a fulcrum with a small white bucket handing on each end. It was not meant for precise measurement but to compare the weight of different items.

The groups were dropping several different objects into the buckets, using trial and error to rank them from lightest to heaviest. There were a variety of things to weigh, including a ping-pong ball, a wooden block, a paper clip, and a small plastic cup. The class was busy and noisy while they completed the

physical science experiment (which we called an "exploration")
and wrote their results down.

That year was my toughest class ever. Our assistant
principal was in the room helping with the exploration. He sat
with a few rowdy boys to help keep them on task. One student in
the group, Gregory, was struggling. He picked up the plastic cup
and the ping-pong ball. After looking at them for a few moments,
he announced, "These remind me of beer pong!" The assistant
principal's eyes grew wide. I'm not sure if he was shocked or
trying not to laugh.

Gregory could barely read. His divorced parents fought
over him. Several times I heard them make shockingly obscene
remarks to and about each other while he stood watching and
listening. He was diagnosed with ADHD, but neither parent
would get him help because it was the *other* parent's fault and
responsibility. He struggled with regular learning connections,
but Greg knew beer pong.

Greg would know afterwards that the cup weighed more than the ball. Plastic cups and ping-pong balls had a relationship he understood. He had obviously seen someone play it. My bigger fear was he had played it himself. He got the comparative weight question right on the test a few days later, which was a miracle for him.

Sometimes things just don't seem relevant to you until much later, when you discover a personal connection. When your class is reading a book about how the moon affects tides, the lesson is relevant only to someone who has seen an ocean. You'd never understand tides unless you've *seen* how it changes the water level. Maybe theoretically you can, but a seven-year-old is not very theoretical. A video could help, I suppose, but personal association is best.

I remember a vocabulary lesson my first year, when I was teaching the word "climate." We had been discussing weather, so I naively hoped that would give the class a clue. "Can anyone tell me what climate means?"

Sally was a student who had been categorized as "a slow learner." She rarely took risks in answering questions, but here she was, enthusiastically waving her hand. I thought she must know if she was so confident.

"Okay, Sally, you tell the class what climate means."

"It's what you do when you see a tree."

I was confused. "When you see a tree?"

Sally rolled her eyes, disgusted with my stupidity. "You see a tree and you *climate!*" she explained, not so patiently.

We had to start over. Even as a first-year teacher, I knew you can't leave an idea that is so mistaken out there or it will come back to haunt you. I had to explain they were spelled differently. One was a verb, the other a noun. We talked about what weather we expect in Chicago in the winter. Then we talked about what winter was like in Mexico and Puerto Rico. We discussed what clothes you would pack if you were traveling to Hawaii or Alaska. Eventually we got to the point that the class understood climate meant the weather we expect for a certain place at a certain time of year. That is, everyone except Sally, who still smugly refused to believe I was correct.

When you teach a topic to a second grader, they will recall it best if it is relevant. Experience is a great teacher. You can take an idea you were trying to make sense of, and then suddenly it comes alive by drawing it or acting it out. An exploration is another wonderful way to build understanding. It can give concrete meaning to air pressure or displacement or whale blubber.

I'm a firm believer in understanding what makes each student tick. I need to know what her strengths are, what she's interested in, or what scares her. If I can do this, then each day is a little bit easier as I can help that child connect to what it is they need to learn. I tortured many student teachers as I forced them to think about each child differently and plan their lessons accordingly.

That is what brings breakthroughs. Sitting at desks all day with a workbook does not work for seven-year-olds. They need to act out whale migration or sing songs about the solar system. When they recognize a pattern or have a physical memory, not only does it make a concept relevant, it helps them retain that new knowledge. The joy of these activities also brings community. Not all learning is academic. Social learning enables us able to function in our world.

During one of my practicum teachings, the classroom teacher I was working with told me, "There are no secrets in here." She was referring to learning. There are very few secrets in a functioning classroom. This does not mean we stand in front of the room and discuss each child's abilities, disabilities, or inabilities. It's something that occurs naturally as we spend hours a day together. Classmates know who can read well, who can draw well, who can do math sums the quickest. They know who struggles to sit still, who has a hard time counting coins. These are not mutually exclusive either. A great reader might not recognize the difference between a nickel or a quarter.

When we know each other well, we can cheer each others' successes honestly. We can ask Wilber to draw the picture while Deedee writes the sentences of the poster. They planned it together. So now both are displaying their own talents.

One of my joyous breakthrough moments wasn't about reading or math. It was about touch.

My darling autistic boy, Taj, loved to run and dance. It was the end of the year and the talent show had been that morning. We were having the class party and Taj was dancing. He was doing a dance move he had seen at the assembly where a line of boys had put their hands on top of each other and made waves with their arms. Taj was standing on the rug with his arms extended, mimicking the dance move. Two girls stood watching him. Finally, one sidled up and asked, "Hey Taj, can we do that with you?" He stopped and looked down. I watched breathlessly. I realized he was smiling.

"Yeah!" he said in his raspy voice as he extended his arms. They laid their hands on his and began to dance together, faces beaming. I was smiling too, but my eyes had filled with tears. His school year was successful because he could let someone touch him while he danced.

I was struggling to find relevancy in my life away from school. I felt I had lost my purpose. While Mark was alive, going through chemotherapy and radiation, undergoing numerous surgeries, and telling bad jokes to hide his pain, my job was to be his cheerleader. I understood my role, my place as the mother of the family. That sounds like something out of the 1950s. Mark and I had a partnership that worked quite well. We agreed to rotate our good cop/bad cop roles when disciplining the kids. Neither of us really liked the bad cop job. He had a passion for cooking and precooked meals for the week on Sunday afternoon. I hadn't chopped an onion in 20 years. We enjoyed each other's company. I had a very full life.

After Mark died, it was as if my team had been disbanded. Elena traipsed through life, but I knew her Pollyanna days were over. Tom was furious at how unfair the world was.

The worst day ever was a couple days after we went to Maine to scatter some of Mark's ashes. Tom, Elena, and I stood in the second floor hallway having a roaring fight. Fights were a rarity in our house, but this one was red hot. I have no recollection of what it was about. Elena got right in Tom's face. "Go ahead, Tom! Hit me! I'm not afraid of you!"

Tom spun on his heel and stormed in his room. I could see how badly he did want to punch her. He slammed his door. Elena and I listened to him *punch, punch, punch* his solid oak door until it splintered and his fist came through.

I remember sitting on the top step and sobbing. All I could think was the insane thought that the property value of the house had dropped because the door would no longer be all original. I was also so afraid for my son. I felt like a failure as a parent.

My second graders made life relevant for me. They gave me a connection with other humans after Mark's death. At home, I frequently treaded on eggshells to avoid upsetting my own kids. My teenagers and I were all trying to find the ways to adjust our behavior and words to rebuild our family without Mark. We

needed to find what was solid enough to be a foundation, what

was light enough for adornments, and what just needed to be

jettisoned. There was a lot a trial and error.

Comments like "This reminds me of beer pong" or "It's

what you do when you see a tree" kept me laughing when so

much laughter had gone out of my life. Their laughter,

excitement, and dancing allowed me to feel unmitigated joy and

delight.

CHAPTER 4

THE GOLDEN RULE AND ME

Each September we began the process of writing the rules. "What rules do you think we need for our class?" I asked my students.

The hands were like popcorn. Everyone was bouncing up and down with an idea. The blurters started shouting out suggestions. The student -teacher sat poised at the chart, ready to record them. I wondered if she could write quickly enough.

Don't hit

Don't kick

Don't slap

Don't bite

No tattling

No stealing someone's toy

No tripping your friends

No tripping anyone

No punching

No running in the halls

No skipping in the hall

Treat everyone nice

No jogging in the hall

No spitting

No picking your nose

No talking in class

The timing for this was planned carefully. Super anal seven-year-olds could blather for days about rules. "Oops!" I'd say in a startled voice. "We have to leave for gym. We'll work on this again tomorrow."

The process moved on. The secret was I knew there would only be three rules. Maybe four. I even knew what the rules would be. It was a plot. I would convince them they would write the rules. The wording would be their choice, but the content would be mine. Like all great ideas, this is not original. These three rules would cover a multitude of sins. The trick was to get the right people to come up with the wording.

"Oh, look! I notice a bunch of these rules are about being safe. Who can think of a rule for being safe?"

I looked around. Skippy, who was always on the go, was bouncing up and down.

"Be safe!" Skippy said.

"What a great idea! Everyone thumbs up if you think this is a great rule."

For that rule, I always called on Skippy, Speedy, or Twinkle Toes.

For the Golden Rule, I pushed them toward the wording. They had all heard it before. It was a rule in kindergarten and first grade. If the first suggestion was, "Be nice to everyone." I would say, "Good idea. Any other suggestions?"

I always called on Snidely or Cruella for this rule. I slowly and painfully pulled the rule suggestion out of them.

It didn't matter who I selected for the final rule of taking care of our things and our school, but if Slobby Robby came up with it, I thought of it as a bonus. My favorite wording for this rule was "Treat our school like it is the White House."

The class signed a board agreeing to follow the rules.

Later in the year, when Skippy crashed into two first graders as he careened full speed down the hall, I reminded him, "What's that rule you wrote about safety? Can you read it to me?"

When Cruella was being wicked and had three, count them, *three* girls in tears, I crossed my arms and calmly looked at her. "Didn't you write that rule about how we treat people? I think your classmates deserve an apology, don't you?"

The Golden Rule is priceless. It reminds us to be our best to others. But at times, it can be hard to understand. Even the teacher (that would be me) forgets sometimes when I am rushed, being bothered by an administrator, overtired, or when it is too stinking hot in the room to breathe. The adult is the role model in a classroom. I do always admit my mistake to everyone who heard me and apologize.

Kids often had a hard time with the Golden Rule. I frequently heard excuses such as, "She hit me first." Harder still was teaching a child what to do when they hadn't mean to hurt someone. I had to model that a lot. If I stepped on a foot as I walked through the room, I made sure I always stopped and said, "Oh, I didn't mean to do that. Are you okay?"

Treating each other like we are all humans makes it easier to remember not to laugh at mistakes. We remember to help someone when they are down (that includes falling). We can recognize each person's strengths. In return, we are willing to take that step out onto a limb and try something new. I cannot count the number of times I have seen students reassure a classmate. They would try not to giggle even when someone makes a tremendous blooper. Their eyes bugged out and their hands slapped over their mouth, but the laughter was stopped.

They could be immeasurably understanding to even the most difficult classmate.

I was always amazed at the joy they received at being part of a group where they could trust each other. Some of my most frustrating moments were the Cruellas and Snidelys bringing someone down. I have seen some very mean children. Most of them could be broken of the habit. As one mother once to me said, "Bullying is not a quality you want your child to have."

The children who couldn't be broken of the habit fell into two groups. First, there was something physiologically wrong. They had no filter and they blurted out what they were thinking. "Yuck, your breath stinks. Don't you brush your teeth?" or "What's wrong with your nose?" It still hurt and was still mean, but these children could usually learn to recognize they have upset someone and sincerely apologize. Most of them could at least learn to be responsible for their actions.

The other group is the children who had parents with the same behaviors. Snippy was one of the meanest boys I have ever taught. His dad treated the lovely, well-educated mom like dirt.

The dad did this in front of teachers, other parents, and his sons.

Her children talked to her that way, too. I once told Snippy while

his mom stood there, "Don't you ever talk to her like that again in

front of me. A mother is the most important person in the world."

His mom looked so startled. I turned to her and said, "I hope you

don't mind."

She replied, "No, that would be nice." I drew a picture of a

thought bubble with "mean words" written in it, drew a red line

through it, and taped it to Snippy's desk. Whenever he got snarky

with his tablemates, I would tap the picture. It helped a little bit.

Stella was the meanest girl I ever taught. She did most of

her terrorizing on the playground. A strikingly beautiful blonde,

Stella was bright but somewhat lazy. She was exceedingly

popular and everyone wanted her to like them. But Stella

excelled at looking down her nose.

I have never had much patience with mean girls. I did not

much like them when I was growing up and have even less

tolerance now. It is as if they have a red glow and I recognize them immediately. Perhaps it is the way they would try to kiss up to me. As a teacher, there is only one diva in my room and it is me.

Stella's favorite classroom trick was to knock a pencil on the floor then look at a classmate with wide staring eyes. She'd then look at the pencil and back at them. She'd repeat that a couple of times. If her classmate didn't pick up the pencil, she'd whisper, "I'll tell Violet that you peed your pants" or something equally horrifying to a second grader. I had several mothers come to complain their daughters were crying themselves to sleep at night, not eating, and not wanting to come to school.

The group she was with was a challenging class. There were well over a dozen learning and behavior problems in the room. Stella didn't pick on the children who had difficulties. Instead, she victimized the little shining diamonds who were hard working, sweet, and easy going—she terrorized the students who were the fresh air of a very smoggy year. It made me nuts. No matter what I tried, I couldn't break her of the habit. She would

just stare at me with her beautiful green eyes whenever she got in

trouble. I ended up taking recess away from her because most of

the behavior was happening then and no one could monitor her

every second. When I talked to her about her behavior, she would

just stare at me unblinkingly.

Her mother complained I was picking on her. She wrote a

very nasty letter to Principal Zelenka about me. The mom walked

in and dropped it on her desk while the principal was sitting there

and walked out. Principal Zelenka called her and scheduled a

meeting for all of us for the next day.

As I walked in the office, Stella's mom gave me a

simpering smile. "Oh, Ms. Meredith, it's so nice to see you." I

almost barfed. What followed was not an easy meeting. She felt I

didn't like her daughter. She felt I embarrassed her daughter

intentionally. I apologized if I had. I explained that her daughter

had no reaction to me, so I was never sure if she was upset,

remorseful, or delighted.

"Oh, that is probably my fault," she replied. "I don't allow her to cry. I just don't have the patience for it."

Chris Zelenka jumped up out of her chair. She came back with handfuls of stuff for counseling. The mom did agree to get help for her Stella. The behavior never actually improved. The following year, she transferred to a different school. I hope things improved for her, but I was not sad to see her transfer. When I heard, I looked around to make sure no children were present. Then I kicked up my heels and did a happy dance in the hall. I am ashamed I did it, but I was so relieved for the other kids that I couldn't contain myself.

Stella never understood the very rule she wrote. I tried, but her mom didn't understand the rule either. It makes it doubly hard to teach. Parents have tons more influence than I do.

In fact, with a bully, and she certainly qualified, I have a hard time treating her in the way I'd like to be treated. I think I'd want someone to teach me to be kind. I would want someone to wake me up and make me treat others in a loving way. Instead,

I'd catch myself bullying her, which just made me more frustrated. I felt so sorry for her in some ways. She never could just be happy.

So the rules are not just for the students; they were for me, also. At least the Golden Rule was. I handled the "Be Safe" and "Be respectful to our school" easily. The Golden Rule is a life lesson. We carry it with us to remind ourselves we can always improve.

CHAPTER 5

LAUGH-LAUGH-LAUGH

Jude came in from the bathroom. "Hey, Lucy! I'm

hooooome!"

I took a deep breath. "Please leave the room and come

back the right way." He did just that. It gave me a chance not to

start laughing with the rest of the people in the room.

Jude also once wrote a story. The story starter (the only

one I ever choose to use) was: *You are walking through the leaves*

on a beautiful fall day. Suddenly you hear a voice in the leaves

shout, "Help!"

Jude wrote: *There was my lost cheeseburger. It had gone away and I couldn't find it. It wanted me to eat it. I love my cheeseburger.*

You try not to laugh at that. Not enough content to get an "A," but funny nonetheless.

Laughter is something that we teachers have to get a tight handle on. I don't mean stopping students from laughing. That would be sad. I mean, stopping yourself from laughing at the students' stunts and absurdities. I frequently have to remind my students, "Second grade isn't a comedy club."

Eleanor would often cause me to lose my restraint. One day, I told my noisy group, "Quiet down, let's get started with math."

"Yeah! We might as well get it over with," Eleanor shouted. Another day, when I gave the sign for the class to stop and listen, she shouted, "Hey! Let the lady talk!"

When you have a class of people who all want your love and attention, laughter keeps all of us moving forward. I'd say to a whiner, "What? Your leg hurts? Let me get my scissors." Or

after another day of three children coming back from recess

holding baggies of ice: "We are depleting the Earth of fresh water

and baggies, people!"

Our school had perfectly lovely banisters. The rails were hip level

for most seven-year-olds. Just raise the haunch an inch or two

and the ride was free. Everyone felt the urge to slide. (I even had

to fight my urges!) Sliding down the rails was not seen as

"responsible" behavior. It was especially irresponsible to do it

when the whole class was lined up in front of you like bowling

pins. My question to anyone I saw doing it was, "Who will want to

put their hand on that railing after your bottom slid on it? Yuck!"

The floors were marble, so the banister slider's landings

needed to be perfect. "Who's going to clean up the blood when

you break your head open?" I'd ask. The slider would look

shocked, but I would be laughing behind my hand.

I sang spelling words: "Jet. I'm leaving on a jet plane. I

don't know when I'll be back again. Oh babe, I hate to go. Jet."

They groaned and laughed at the same time. I also found songs that reminded me of them and serenaded each student with his or her song. One boy always had a cheese bagel sandwich for lunch. His song was, "The Boogey-Woogey Bagel Boy of Room 203."

Laughter is a great disciplinarian. My absolute best threat was a lipstick kiss on the cheek, à la grandma. I would take out a tube of lipstick from my desk drawer, pocket, or purse. This usually brought a gasp from the class. They knew what was coming.

"I noticed, Calvin (or whomever), you're not doing your work," I'd say, taking the top off and slowly twisting the tube upwards. I'd apply lipstick to my bottom lip.

"I sure hope ..." I then put lipstick on the right side of my top lip.

"...you have started..." Next the left side.

"...your math. I'd hate..." I rubbed my lips together. At this point everyone in the room had scrambled to do whatever they needed to be doing.

"...to have to give you a big ol' kiss on the cheek." I looked up and around. Everyone was on task.

No student was exempt from my lipstick trick. I could silence a bus of rowdy kids simply by showing them how many tubes of lipstick I had in my purse. The funny thing was they loved to hate it. Sometimes secretly, they came to me with a cheek tilted upward and asked me to give them a kiss.

Sometimes you'd get a child who laughs at everything, like Elmer. If someone just glanced at him, he laughed. This was a tough problem to solve. Was that joy bubbling up? Was it a lack of self-control? Was he a fairy changeling?

I called Elmer over to talk quietly to him. It wasn't a soft, low laugh—he bellowed.

"Can you please try some self-control?" I asked. "I feel like I'm calling your name all the time and having to stop the class while you calm down. That can't be fun for you."

"It was fun until you made me stop," he complained.

Laughter welled up in both grandiose and tiny ideas. It occurred because we had the ability to recognize the absurd in everyday moments. It could have been a slapstick moment or a bad joke. It could have been one of those hilarious misunderstandings which were as convoluted as "Who's on First?" We laughed many times each day, keeping the mundane at bay. My mother always claims it is better to laugh than cry. When we find ourselves doing both, it's truly a soul cleansing moment.

One year, a first-grade teacher came to me and informed me that one of her student's parents requested me as their son's teacher for second grade. She is a good friend of mine, but she was concerned this little boy, who had been diagnosed with

Asperger's, wouldn't get my sense of humor or my sarcasm.

But as it turned out, we got along famously. I discovered

he loved outlandish vocabulary words like "fewmets" or

"chimera." I knew I no longer had to worry that he might

misunderstand me when he walked up to me one day with one

eye shut. "Guess what I am?"

"A one-eyed pirate?" I guessed.

"No!" he harrumphed. "A cyclops!" He then proceeded to

laugh so hard he could hardly breathe. His joke wasn't ready for

Comedy Central, but his joy at being able to tell a joke filled me

with wondrous delight.

I am sure there were a few days without laughter in my

room, but I don't really recollect any. There is a teacher saying

that goes, "Never let them see you smile until November." I

would go bonkers.

Instead, I remind my students if we work hard, we will

have plenty of time for fun. I laughed at my own mistakes. I read funny poems before lunch or even better, scary poems that make us laugh at how we jump. I talked with crazy accents or voices. My class loved my terrible French accent or my fake brogue. The kids rolled their eyes in fake horror when I used my muted preschool teacher voice, "Now boys and girls, come sit with your friends." That was baby talk in their minds. They loved my "whiny voice," but it gave me a headache to talk like that *and* to have to listen to it.

Sometimes they didn't realize what they said was funny. I had an exceptionally bright group of boys one year who could spell any word I gave them. I got them a set of unabridged dictionaries to peruse. These lads were not only smart but fairly ornery. A tattler ran over and told me Joel was looking up "bad words." I called Joel over. He was the smarty pants who had the misfortune of being caught although I knew there were a couple other guilty parties. They sat watching to see what the outcome would be. "I know you are smart, Joel, but I didn't get you those dictionaries to get you in trouble. If you know it's a bad idea, why did you do it?"

"I just don't understand it. It's like a whole different side of my personality comes out when I see those bad words." He looked like he was going to cry. I had to swallow my laughter. I still shake my head and wonder what side of Joel's personality is going to come out when he's a teenager.

I had been married to a man who had made me laugh every day. He saw the zany in most situations and just making eye contact with him sometimes would crack me up. The first night we met was a snowy winter evening and we were riding the El train home together after a money and banking class at the American Institute of Banking. He was wearing these thick-soled leather hiking boots. He had asked me a question that made me pause before I answered. He then pointed at the boots.

"I'm sorry," he said. "I wear these big old waffle stompers to put in my mouth. Open mouth. Insert foot." Maybe it was the words, maybe it was the delivery, but I laughed. And I never stopped.

He made jokes as he lay dying in the hospital and then in our living room. We both had learned from a friend who had died years earlier that you live until you die. Mark kept living until it grew to be too much. The last few days were horrible, as his eyes rolled in a morphine-induced stupor. No jokes then. We just muddled through those days. The final joke came, though.

We stood counting by 5s to 100. Then we would start over. Elena kept making mistakes through her tears. Mark looked at me, a little frustrated by it. I winked at him with a half smile. He nodded at me. I held one of his hands, Elena the other. Tom stood next to his sister. Pie, our huge orange cat, lay between his legs.

Mark's morphine had been out for a few hours at this point and we were doing what I called "Mommy Lamaze." It was keeping your mind focused on something else to distract you from the pain. Skip counting or saying your ABCs was a wonderful trick for skinned knees. This, however, was life-ending pain.

The useless substitute hospice nurse had shown up at 7:45 a.m. after she had called me at 6 a.m. to ask directions to our house from the suburbs. I told her to ask someone else.

Her hand shook as she refilled the morphine pump. *Too little, too late*, I thought.

When the kids got up that morning, I told them there would be no school. This was it.

As Mark took his last breaths, we all were saying, "I love you, Daddy." "I love you, Dad." "Go to your beautiful place, Mark. I will love you forever."

As Mark took his last breath, my children and I stood holding his hands. Chopin played on the stereo. Suddenly, the overpowering sound of a waterfall filled the room. The music had switched to an incredibly loud waterfall CD. We all laughed through our tears. I rushed to turn it off. Who knew I was turning

off the laughter that had filled my home for so long?

Thank heavens for seven-year-old laughter that saved my

life.

CHAPTER 6

WHAT I LOVE

Emmett was a quirky, troubled boy. He was probably bipolar. He could be bubbly, charming, and chatty. In a flash, he would become moody, aggressive, and deeply self-hating. I adored him. My head is still full of the Emmettness of him. Once he asked me if I knew why he liked money.

"No, why?"

The wiry, seven-year-old ball of energy replied, "Because I can buy things for my kids with it."

"You have kids?"

"*No!*" he moaned. "I have to get married and my wife has to get pregnant and then I'll have kids."

"Go sit down," I told him, shaking my head.

Chuckling, he started to walk away, then turned around. "But first I have to find a wife."

I never sat at my desk. Instead, the space under my desk was a place decorated with posters of Van Gogh's room, a Renoir garden, and a seaside painting. We called it the supply desk. Under the desk there was a pink box full of lavender scented pigs, a little pillow with "Breathe" stitched upon it, a bluebird puppet, and sometimes a stress ball, although these had a tendency to be destroyed. Inside the lid of the box it said:

1. Breathe.

2. Count to sixty.

3. Breathe again.

Another bipolar student had helped me fill the box and decorate the space. Any stressed-out student could ask to sit there. My class called it "the Stress Box." I often wondered what parents must have wondered about me letting a child sit in a box.

Emmett often relaxed there until he lost the privilege in a very

Emmett way.

One day, Alicia Lee, the first-grade teacher, was observing

me give a lesson. The class sat on the rug, listening. My student

teacher was working one on one with someone at her table.

Emmett was super antsy so I was letting him calm down under

my desk. He had been agitated and I was hoping a little quiet

time would help him settle back into his charming self. Alicia was

sitting next to the desk in a chair about a foot away from him.

Suddenly, Frank DeJohns, the third grade teacher, stuck

his head in the door. "Is Emmett supposed to be running down

the hall into the auditorium balcony?"

I asked Frank to buzz the office to let them know what

happened. The school went on Emmett alert. This meant several

adults were watching the doors to make sure he didn't leave the

building while one or two tried to locate him to make sure he

didn't hurt himself. If you got too close to him, he barreled off in

another direction, so the goal was to keep him within sight.

I was baffled as to how he had managed to escape the room. Later, we realized that he had pried off the back of the metal supply desk and army crawled out of the room under the student desks. He had silently pushed crates and chairs out of his way. He accomplished this with three adults in the room.

This situation made me crazy. I was worried for his safety. I was worried how his behavior affected his classmates, who were always excited to announce, "Guess what Emmett did today?" to their parents. Mostly it made me crazy because I loved him and was unsure how to save him.

In fact, I love them all. I love even, and maybe especially, the really naughty ones. I told them a million times, "Once you are my student, you are always my student. I will be watching you." They saw it when older students dropped by to visit (willingly) or were sent to finish some work or take an in-school suspension. A student is mine forever.

I was lucky. I was able to teach who I love. I love second graders. Here is what I love about them.

I love the laughter and the tears. There are more tears from boys at this age than girls. The tears flow without restraint. They hiccup, their eyes fill and brim over, and then they throw themselves into your arms—crying as if the world might end. Boys usually cry more from the spirit, their essence, their center than the girls. Only the tough girls really cry from the spirit.

I love the tough girls, the little mamas. The bossy ones, the pushy ones, and the know-it-alls fill me with delight. I love them as long as they can stop to listen sometimes. I love them as long as they have compassion wrapped in the bossiness. I marvel at their brazen behavior. I believe the world would not run as smoothly without those grown up bossy girls who have become bossy women.

I love the shy ones. Much to everyone's surprise, they will one day find their voice. I'll hear a little tiny girl who has barely spoken above a whisper say in a loud, clear voice: "Hey! You can't do that to us!" or "Leave her alone!" or "My way would work too if you gave it a chance." Then I feel my arm pump. Yes!

I love the holes in paper and the frustrated tears. They occur hand in hand—eraser holes, frustration, and tears. Seven-year-olds want to be perfect, but they are still learning. Patience with themselves is something they need to learn. Second graders need to practice calming breaths over and over. I reassured them with lists of my own mistakes and how I learned from them.

I'm an expert on seven-year-olds. Thirteen years of teaching hundreds of those bright beings make me shake my head in wonder.

I love their teeth, either wiggling or missing or humongous adult-sized teeth in a little face. I've reached in and pulled out a few bloody, wiggly ones. The trick is to turn a baggie inside out and put your hand in it. Quickly, hide it behind your back. Have them close their eyes or look up to the ceiling. Moving like the speed of light, reach in and give the tooth a yank. It's best if they don't anticipate it, but that's hard to accomplish. One beautiful girl would stop by each year to remind me of the day I stealthily pulled her tooth. Every time she visited, we laughed together over her shock and my delight. I had other teachers send students to my room, notes in hand requesting I pull their tooth, *please*. After all, wiggly teeth become a classroom distraction especially when it includes blood.

Once the tooth is between your fingers, turn the baggie right side out and zip it shut. Have the student put it in her bookbag on the way to the drinking fountain to rinse out her mouth.

Later in the year (December usually), I read Kate DiCamillo's book, *Because of Winn Dixie,* to the class. When we come to that beautifully poignant line about how missing her mama is like putting a tongue in the spot where you've lost a tooth, I pause. She explains that you know it is gone but you can still expect it to be there. I read that line a couple of times. We discussed it. I would gush, "Isn't it wonderful how she describes it? We all know that feeling. I love this image. Here I'll read it again." The seven-year-olds wisely agreed. Yes, by seven we have all lost something that was a part of us, even if it is simply a tooth.

Seven-year-olds are funny. Their humor is honed. Their jokes are often still immature but they are trying. Joke books are extremely popular. I have way too much of a tendency toward sarcasm. So I would comment to a group of girls at the tissue box, "Five at a time? Is this Snot Fest?" They always laughed and sat down.

Oh, the hugs! Some children are stealth huggers, sneaking up behind you. Some boys have already perfected the one arm hug. Some just threw their arms wide and wrapped them around me. I hugged back with a passion and never hugged without asking first. "Could you use a hug right now?"

Sevens are the most eager learners a teacher could ever dream about. They are like sponges. They have a lot to learn and they know it. They run after the knowledge and grab at it like candy being tossed at a 4th of July parade. Academics and social behavior are both soaked up and guzzled down. A favorite phrase of mine was, "This is a life skill." Whenever I uttered it, they leaned forward waiting for the secret to be imparted. Ah, the elixir of life for a teacher.

Sevens think they are mini adults. They know they are kids, but they want to be adults. It is their goal. They are way more mature than tweens who aren't sure who they are. Seven-year-olds know.

This is also the age of horrible accidents. They think if they see someone drowning, they can jump in and save them. They forget they don't know how to swim. Thank the stars I never had this happen to a student of mine.

I taught what I loved and loved what I taught. It is a beautiful thing.

CHAPTER 7

WHAT'S THE NATURE OF YOUR MALAJUSTMENT?

"What is the nature of your maladjustment?" was my father's favorite question. He asked it whenever one of his six children was in a tiff for no apparent reason. He loved this question. It gave him great glee to utter it. In fact, I think he wanted someone to be moody or dramatic just so he could announce the query.

This question might make you wonder if my dad was sophisticated or learned. No. He was charming, charismatic, and smart but not learned. He would probably have told you he was a country boy. He thought of himself that way although his father was a profitable car dealer.

He also claimed he was "the pickle in the middle with the mustard on top," meaning he was number four of seven kids. He was the second of three boys, also. He had been a crazy boy at school, a mediocre student who was probably dyslexic. Even in his speech he turned around his "m" and "n." He said Walt Dismey or Motre Dane instead of Notre Dame.

My mother is the bookish one. She is very smart. Her parents were well educated, and to sit with the adults at parties, you simply had to be competent enough to insert puns into everyday conversation.

My dad didn't seem to be much of a reader. Not compared to my mother. She finished the complete Readers' Digest Condensed Books set in less than a week. Looking back, my dad did read a lot: the paper, National Geographic, little devotional books. He read the "funnies" daily.

On the comic pages, there was a box about two inches by three inches titled "Word of the Day." I didn't realize until I was an adult that my dad "studied" it each day. It had a word with a standard definition and a cartoon illustrating how the word was used. It said something like, "Use it three times and it's yours."

One of my pet peeves is when people talk down to children. Well, anyone for that matter, but kids in particular. A child has life experience. It might be just a few years but for them it is their whole life. For us, a month is quick and over in a flash. For a seven-year-old, a month is something like 1/80 of their life experience. A school day lasts forever, even for us sometimes. Summer seems endless.

While baby talk is horrible, in my opinion, it's worse to assume they know nothing in life either. When I would read *Because of Winn Dixie* every year to my class, we would pay attention to the list of 10 things India Opal's daddy listed about the momma who abandoned them. One of the items on the list was that her momma drank. My sage seven-year-olds nodded their heads. They knew demon rum is a problem, whether from their own family experience or a neighbor.

We watched the movie after we finished the book. They sat with notebooks and took notes. They compared how the movie was like the book and how was it different. The drinking was left off Daddy's list in the movie. The class, every single year, was disgusted. They weren't anyone's fools. They knew it was left out because "people" thought they were too young. They ranted and raved, complaining it was a lack of respect.

I've had students whose parents have abandoned them, whose families physically fought with each other, or whose parent abused another parent. Some of my students had siblings die. Children don't live in a vacuum, but the real world.

I've hooked kids up with other kids with similar family situations. I introduced Margaret and Bridget. The girls both had a younger sibling die. Margaret, two years older, saw it as her job to check in on Bridget. It didn't happen often, but understanding they weren't alone mattered to both girls.

One year, I had four kids whose parents were getting or had just gotten divorced. I gave permission for them to just bend each other's ears if they needed someone to listen. No questions asked by me. All they needed to do was request, "Can I take so-and-so out to the hall?" Off they wandered. They returned a few minutes later, chatting. One student usually had red-rimmed eyes from crying.

Each morning, the class came to the rug, sitting cross-legged, chattering with their friends. Every day, I asked my class to close their eyes and wish for a "great" day. Silence fell. Eyes would shut. Bodies became taunt. Some children even made the sign of the cross. I never asked what their wishes were. It was enough they were making them. I sent my wishes winging upwards also. I joked to other adults that this was prayer in school. Whether it was or not, it signaled the fresh beginning of a new day leaving our out of school problems behind.

Human compassion, as well as a sense of humor, can get a child to take risks to learn. Children need to learn we all have issues with which to deal. By seven, the pressure is on to succeed. The pressure to get ready for the tests in third grade is building.

We call third grade a "benchmark year" in Chicago public schools. In other words, if you don't pass those tests, you repeat third grade. I once heard the idea that the prison industry looked at third grade test scores to determine future need for jail cells. I have no idea if it's true, but failing a grade after age eight does increase a child's chance of dropping out.

Can I just say here that I think testing in this manner is wrong? Finland, whose educational outcomes are shown off around the world, doesn't test like we do. Instead, they focus on individual student strengths. They support areas where a student needs to grow.

I don't mind all tests. But they need to be viewed as one of many forms of assessment. I like tests for determining what students need to learn. For example, if a test showed most of my class didn't understand "story setting," then I taught it. We figured out the where and when of a story by discussing it during read-alouds. We created mini dioramas for the books we read.

Sometimes test questions are just beyond seven-year-old ability. Here is an example:

A boy has to read a book that is 162 pages long. On Monday, he read 47 pages. On Tuesday, he read 36 pages. On Wednesday, he read 39 pages. How many more pages does he need to read to finish the book? If he has to finish reading the book on Friday, make a plan for him to complete the book.

This question was given in September of second grade. To get a "4," the top score, a child had to solve how many more pages needed to be read. That was 2 points. He had to identify the unit (pages) for another point. The final point was the mathematical equation for the plan to complete reading the book.

Students don't learn to do double-digit addition or subtraction until the second marking period of second grade. Arthur, however, came up with the correct number of pages to be read: 40. He didn't write "pages," so he lost a point. He had a plan to finish the book though: *Turn off the TV. Put away the Game Boy. Sit down and focus. It's not that much to read!*

He only got 2 points on the problem, but I thought he should have earned a bonus point for his brilliant answer.

One day I asked my dad about the "nature of your maladjustment" phrase. I was probably in my late twenties at the time. He started laughing so hard that he turned red. He explained how he studied the "Word of the Day" each day. One day the word was "maladjustment." He explained, "Here was this shrink asking a man on the couch, 'What's the nature of your maladjustment?' I could picture each one of you guys laying on that couch and I was the shrink. There are a lot of crazy people in this house!" He wiped the tears from his eyes.

I laughed with him. I learned my dad saw the humor in the nuttiness around him. I also was surprised to realize he worked every day to improve himself. He told me another time he wasn't much of a reader as a kid, but he enjoyed it later. "I read so slow, but I like it."

I have students for whom reading was never easy. Will they be like my dad? Will they be able to sing the songs they heard once in a movie or on a television show? Will they look at a diagram once and be able to put something together? Will they read charts well enough to be the #1 warrantee man for Chrysler one year as he was? Will they remember jokes and deliver them flawlessly?

My dad was intelligent. He wasn't rich or powerful. He was smart in a do-it-yourself sort of way. He worked two jobs his whole adult life. He was Santa for organizations at Christmas and a precinct captain in town. He worked hard as a Young Democrat and at the Moose. He didn't drink much—a beer after mowing the lawn. "Eight ounces. Cold from the fridge," he'd say. He had traveled far and wide in the navy. He loved my mom in spite of her moodiness. He had more friends than he could count.

When I think about the test scores we put on these kids, I think how my father would have fared. When we look at these test scores, we assign the child a number. Will that number designate how productive that child will be? Will it predict if they will be hard working? Does it indicate kindness or creativity? Does it show if they will vote as adults? Is future happiness or self-satisfaction or dedication determined?

Just like my father, each child is a light. We cannot simply determine the gifts they have to offer the world through their ability to take a test. I think it is maladjusted.

CHAPTER 8

DECISIONS, DECISIONS

It is our choices, Harry, that show what we truly are, far more
than our abilities.

—J.K. Rowling

I always joked that I was Room 20ADHD. I never had a

class without a serious wiggler. Frequently, it was four or five.

One year, I had over ten! It meant I had to have devices that

helped each one. What worked for Ellie didn't necessarily work

for Calvin or Greg.

Let me explain before you wonder if I'm maligning these

wonderfully energetic kids. Sometimes children have an official

Attention Deficit Hyperactive Disorder diagnosis. Sometimes

they don't. Sometimes they've never been assessed. I've had

children with lead poisoning, which can cause hyperactivity and learning issues. I've had some who had poor diet or sleep habits. I've had some with a preliminary diagnosis of being bipolar. Sensory integration issues can also cause the inability to settle down or, as I like to say, "to be comfortable in their own skin." It doesn't really matter which it is. They all need help finding a way to accomplish learning and not to feel as if they were social outcasts.

What did work for Calvin was a puppet that looked like a basket of five puppies. Each puppy needed one finger. He also used a "kick band," a yoga band tied around the base of his chair. He would sit in his chair and bounce his heels against it at a rapid pace. He probably kicked the equivalent of five miles a day.

The kick band worked miracles for many kids. It is a tool suggested for children with sensory integration issues, but I found my wigglers used it the most. Not all did though. Some just trampled it onto the floor. One boy pulled his up right under the seat on his chair and strummed it like a bass. *Bump, bump, bump.*

For these kids, choice about behavior has to be stressed and stressed again until you suddenly find some trick that works. The wigglers have to be part of the decision-making process.

Me: I see you are having a hard time not touching your classmates at the rug. Do you like it when people touch you?

Ellie: No! I want to smack them when they touch me.

Me, inwardly sighing: What can I do to help you stop?

Ellie, with a dramatic shrug: I dunno!

Me: Would you like to try sitting in a chair next to the student teacher? Do you think that might work? Or do you want to sit near your desk?

Ellie: I'll sit next to the student teacher.

Later that day, while the student teacher was busy with something more pressing, Ellie discovered she could scoot the chair, with much screeching, close enough to make her foot reach someone's bottom. *Poke, poke, poke.*

Okay, that choice didn't work. Time for Plan B or Plan ZZ, since we had already tried dozens of things. We'd keep trying until something clicked and Ellie could abstain from irritating her classmates.

For some kids, a stress ball works until another ADHD student signals he's ready to catch the ball. There it goes zinging over the rest of the class. Self-restraint isn't a wiggler's strong suit. So, yet again, we discuss the reason throwing the ball wasn't a great plan. The ball goes back in my drawer and, once again, we try something else.

Sometimes giving choices when you ask a question can backfire in unexpected ways. Paval (one of my genius boys) and Carmen, a quiet little girl, had spent a month in Mexico extending their winter break by a few weeks. I was quite concerned about the Carmen because she was a struggling student who had a lot of language confusion. I sat down next to them at lunch one day and asked Carmen if she was dreaming in Spanish, English, or both. I was concerned her language confusion might have gotten even worse. The girl answered, "Spanish." I was actually relieved

that the answer was one or the other and not Spanglish.

Deciding I better be fair, I then turned to Paval. "And you?

Do you dream in Spanish or English?" He replied dramatically

with a continental shrug in his best accent, "Me? I dream in *ze*

French."

Choice is a fine thing. We all like choice. What ice cream to

pick, what shoes to wear, which book to read. As a girl, my family

would go out to eat. This was rare as there were six kids. I would

look at the menu and usually picked grilled cheese. Each of my

sisters perused the menu. Peggy would order spaghetti, Nora, a

cheeseburger. Linda would cry every time because there were too

many choices. She wanted it all.

I learned the parental choice strategy early. You can have

water or milk to drink. You can pick up your toys then play

outside with Timmy or you can sit in that chair all morning. Okay,

probably not that drastic. This technique generally worked.

Sometimes they picked things that I wouldn't have chosen, so I knew it meant they didn't want the "real" choice. If my daughter Elena said she'd rather take a time out instead of making her bed so I'd let her go to Lena's house, I knew something was up. I learned never to give anything as a choice that I wasn't willing to let them do or follow through with.

As a teacher, I tried to give as much choice as possible in a room of 20-plus kids. In a classroom, the choice could be, you can sit *there* or *there*. You can be quiet during fire drills or you can give up recess. You can have white or chocolate milk. Simple. Sometimes you gave bigger choices such as you can do any of these projects on your story. You can do any page you want. You can sort these coins however you'd like.

"Sit still or lose free time" is a horror for a child whose body chemistry doesn't allow it, whether it is caused by ADHD, lack of sleep, or no breakfast. It's not a choice; it's torture. It's as if you said, "You worthless imp! No free time!" Sitting still isn't an option within their ability.

I made the choice to keep working after Mark died. I had missed a lot of time at the beginning of the school year before his death. I needed to be there afterwards. My heart was so sad, but that choice kept me moving forward.

I had a particularly tough group that year. Even if I had been there every single day, they would not have formed a cohesive "safe" group. It was a class of outliers. My sister, Ellen, figured God gave me that untamed group to keep me from dwelling on my worries and my loss. Perhaps. I just know I chose to go in to school. I fought their bad habit of stealing each other's stuff. I fought their meanness to each other. I fought their total disregard for limits. It gave me a mission and a purpose.

Much of that year is a blur. I chose to be in the classroom. I can't really say if I made good choices at home. I felt like my world was tumbling down. My son couldn't stand to see or hear me cry, so I did all my crying in the car. We ate pizza four nights a week. I was unbearably, decidedly alone.

I kept having dreams Mark was really still alive and we couldn't decide what to do with the insurance money. Usually we were sitting in bed in some sweet B&B full of morning sunlight. Sometimes we were taking a walk along a river path in a city or park.

"How will we tell them you're not dead?" I'd ask.

"Why do they think I'm dead?"

"I'm not sure. You were so sick. I guess they all thought you must have died."

"Can we give the insurance money back, do you suppose? Will we be arrested for fraud if we keep it? I'm still sick, after all."

"The money is horrid, Mark. I'd rather have you any day. It feels like blood money. Let's just send it back."

The daylight from my eastern-facing windows and the radio set off by my alarm would bring me back to Earth and the land of waking. The realization Mark was not next to me every morning, the idea of him being alive just moments ago, was oh so wrong. It drove me out of bed.

So I got up and went to work. To my crazy, chaotic haven.

My harbor. Where the unexpected was expected.

CHAPTER 9

BACK IN THE DAY

When I was in second grade, the morning of October 5 was crazy. My mom was in labor with her fifth child. I would tell my class each year about the chaos occurring as I got on the school bus. Linda had to dress her paper dolls to take with her to my cousins' house. She said Aunt Dorothy didn't like naked paper dolls. Peggy had her shoes on the wrong feet, but her legs were crossed so my dad couldn't tell. One-year-old Nora had lost her shoe and was chewing on her sock. When I told the story to the class, I was hoping my sister would be born in the car like my classmate Betty Jo Conlon's sister was just a week earlier. My dad was trying to get everyone out the door exactly so that wouldn't

happen.

At recess, a boy came and told me a lady was by the fence

and wanted to talk to me. It was a smiling Aunt Dorothy. "Lee-

Ann, you have a new baby sister, Ellen Therese. I thought you

would want to know. Your dad said to tell you she looks just like

you." I felt all warm inside. Each year, I told the class, it was one

of the best days of my life because I got my sister Ellen.

They can relate to this story. Second graders know about

babies being born. They don't know the process but they

understand the baby is in the mom and then it comes out, usually

at the hospital. Then there is this wiggly, squirmy, tiny baby who

keeps them awake at night. Later, the same baby will mess with

their toys and scribble on the homework. Homework is far more

likely to be eaten by a baby sister or brother than the dog.

My "When I Was Seven" stories were always a big hit with

my class. I wrote and told stories of back in the day often. Did

they actually all happen that year? Not all. A few were when I was six or eight. They did all happen, although my mom or sister

Linda, twenty months younger than I, might recall them

differently.

For Mothers' Day, when I was in second grade, I gave my

mom two ducklings from our neighbor's farm. She wasn't thrilled.

My dad thought it was hysterical. The ducks were two different

breeds. The Pekin duck had the standard orange bill and feet. The

other was a Muscovy duck, which had a pink bill and feet. These

two little homeless ducklings bonded. Even after we sent them

back to the farm because they filled our yard with poop, you

would find a Peking and a Muscovy wandering around together.

BFFs.

Another classic story was the day I ran away from home. I

was furious about something. When I told my mom I was running

away, she offered to help me pack and handed me a paper

grocery bag. She must have been furious. I left barefoot. I

stomped through the fallow field to the neighbors' farm, where I

was sure they would love and understand me. I stepped on a stick that suddenly moved. I looked down to see a green snake. *Bam!* I was on my way home, screaming, "Mommy!"

Another time, we lost my younger sister Peggy and found her buried in the hall closet under blankets taking a nap. Yet another story involved me breaking my arm after I fell out of a baby buggy being pulled by a pony at the same neighbors' farm. The kids loved the story of when my teenage neighbor girl passed out on me on the school bus when she had an epileptic seizure. I, however, thought she had died. Once I filled the water reservoir in my play kitchen with milk. That story has a stinky ending.

One of the classes' favorite stories was when my little sister Peggy started screaming in her sleep. Linda, not very patiently, said, "Peggy! Stop it!"

"There's a lion in my bed!"

"Peggy, there is no lion in your bed. Go back to sleep," I told her in my best big sister voice.

"There's a lion in my bed!" she screamed.

My mom came in the room. "What in heaven's name is going on?"

"There's a lion in my bed!" Peggy screamed again.

Mom sat on the edge of the bed. "Honey, there is no lion. I'll sit with you and you go back to sleep."

"There's a lion in my bed!" she continued screaming.

"For crying out loud!" The bedroom lights snapped on and my dad was standing in the door. My dad was a sweet man, but he was grumpy, grumpy, grumpy if you woke him up.

"There's a lion in my bed!" she screamed again.

"Peggy Margaret Schutz, there is no lion in this room. I'll look under the bed." Dad looked under the bed.

"There's a lion *in* my bed!" she screamed.

My mom sighed and pulled back the covers. What do you think was there? A cat, a stuffed animal, a Barbie?

"How on earth did this potato get in your bed?" Mom asked in an incredulous voice.

"Maybe the lion left it." Peggy said as she rolled over and went back to sleep.

My students referred to this story as "The Potato Story." It was one of their favorites and was frequently requested.

One of my boys once told me I had such an exciting life. I never thought it was particularly unusual. For the most part, my parents just laughed at the messes we made and the games we played.

While these stories helped my students be better writers, it also helped them relate to me. It reminded me again and again of how it feels to be in second grade. The seven-year-old stories grounded us, turning us into humans who have something in common. Lonely me, I found it perfectly lovely to connect to another spark of humanity.

CHAPTER 10

BEING AN IDEALIST IS HARD WORK

I heard Juanita crying. It was September. We were cutting out number triangles from the back of our math workbooks. While my experience with Juanita was still new, she didn't strike me as a sobber. I walked over. "What's going on?"

"Sergio keeps telling me to cut my hair. He is snapping his scissors at me. My mom will be real mad if I cut it." She plopped her head down on her desk and cried dramatically.

I resisted the urge to roll my eyes. I looked at Sergio. He had that "I won't blink so she'll think I'm innocent" eye-popping stare. I crossed my arms and gave Sergio the teacher glare. I knew I could wait him out.

"Well, her bangs are too long." Sergio was a petite, curly-haired fashionista. He was very artistic and drew dresses in his spare time. Her long bangs probably did bother him, but that was too bad.

Holding my hand out, I said, "Give me your scissors."

"Why?"

"If you don't remember how we use scissors in our room, you need to take a break from using them. The first person done cutting out their number triangles will cut out yours."

He very begrudgingly handed me the scissors. He sat with his arms crossed, pouting at his desk for the next half hour. He had pouting down to a science.

As I mentioned before, the beginning of the year is tai chi second grade. We start with a slow, steady pace. We review pencils, then crayons, how we store things, and how we use them. Every year someone like Sergio has to have a friend cut their work out for them because they don't follow the scissor rules. It takes weeks to start moving at a medium pace. By

Halloween, however, you can let partners reading at a similar range pick an appropriate Halloween book, and tell them to practice a page to read aloud to the class. They are tasked with making a poster about their story, first a sloppy copy, then a final draft. When they are done, they read their selection to the class in their spookiest voices and then the poster.

Being an idealist isn't the easiest way to live. It is much easier to open a book that gives instructions and follow them. Or have the class open a workbook and say, "Do page 37." I've tried both of those routes. I always ended up driving off-road in about a week. I mean, week six of second grade the basal spelling list included "coincidence," a word I can barely spell. Whose idea was that? Many of them don't even know what the word means. That's the other thing—why give them words to spell when they don't know the meaning? Most beginning second graders can read the word "din" but how many know what it means. They usually think they are having a dyslexic moment and that the word must be "bin."

I believe children learn best by doing. So, given a basal, I rewrite it immediately. Why were these stories put in this order? Which story can I tie into social studies or science? Can I use the story to teach the comprehension strategy I committed to teaching this month? Will the students find this story interesting, compelling, and relevant? How can I teach a story I hate? What's the point? The kids will know within minutes how I feel about the story.

I became known for finding stories that tied units up in a bow. I love literature so searching for books is a joy and passion. The class either laughed or moaned when I held up a story they hadn't heard before and exclaimed, "This is one of my all-time favorite books!" I have hundreds of favorite books.

That is part of the idealism. I had to show them that it is okay to love books, science, and poetry—whatever it may be. The excitement of looking through an index of a book on whales, discovering the pattern of leaves matches the math problem, or realizing the poem they love doesn't rhyme—this is the bread of a

teacher's diet.

By December, they are writing their own chapter books

about whales (They only need three sentences per chapter topic.)

They chose how to earn 100 points on whale projects. Then I was

busy, teaching them to draw a whale, showing them how to

make a mobile, or how to make a planner for their book. The

projects filled the room. The books brought tears of frustration,

laughter, and puffed out chests.

I read somewhere we learn 75 percent of what we need to

succeed in school by the end of second grade. The rest is gravy. I

believe this. They have to be able to read fluently, add and

subtract, understand the concept of multiplication and division,

and write complete sentences. This is hard work, learning these

things. As adults, we have forgotten how tricky English is. There

are three ways to spell the sound "to." It isn't spelled

phonetically. And math! We forget that adding and subtracting

multiple digits is very confusing, especially subtraction

Sergio, my little fashionista, was a great reader. His reading group was reading a book about inventors. He just couldn't wrap his mind around the word "prototype." The rest of the group came up with the image of building a model. He still didn't get it. Finally, I explained.

"Let's say you are creating a wedding gown." He nodded. "You don't want to waste that beautiful lace and silk until you are certain the design will hang right. So you use fabric you might use for sheets and sew the dress out of it. That's a prototype."

He lifted his hands out from his sides. "Oh, I get it." The word prototype showed up in his writing the rest of the year.

What I love about seven- and eight-year-olds is their joy for learning. Their brains are bottomless pits. You just open up their minds, stick a funnel in, and start pouring in the oil of knowledge. Some kids have narrow funnels and things get stuck. They are the ones that require a different angle or a slower pouring. Some kids don't even need the funnel: the faster you pour it, the quicker they absorb it. Most kids are somewhere in between.

In March, we studied famous women. Students paired up again to create projects from the biographies they read. One popular project choice was to create a treasure box with six objects that represented their famous woman's life. Sergio's partner was disgusted with him, as Sergio had difficulty finding time to work on his project. He was too busy helping his classmates create dresses to go in their women's treasure box. I got him to agree to draw sketches of the dresses during free time. Then his classmates could make the dresses themselves.

There is a saying that a teacher knows things are going right when the teacher has nothing to do while students are working. It's true. But that ease comes after much preparation. If you take the time, sometimes slowly and methodically, sometimes layering lessons, sometimes practicing bits and bits and bits, then you can let go of the kite string and watch them fly.

By June, during author studies, the children open up the craft cupboard, discuss project choices with a partner, plan, create, clean up, and share what they have created. They are learning every minute. It has become who they are as students. It's not just the reading and comprehension, which is important, but also the problem-solving skills, negotiating skills, and decision-making skills that develop.

That was simply joy, joy, joy. I ran down the hall to find another adult to watch what was happening in my room. That was the payoff for a year's worth of hard work.

I proudly showed their first-grade teachers what the former first graders, a year later, have accomplished. I shared with my grade level team. I dragged middle school teachers in to look. Yes, I taught them, but I was proud of their hard work. I was just as awed by my low readers beautiful diorama as I was by the intricate character scrapbook my top students created. As you would expect, Sergio's was breathtaking.

CHAPTER 11

WHAT YOU CAN LEARN FROM A MEATBALL

A few days before school starts, we ask parents to bring in their child to be evaluated. One year, a girl arrived with her mom and baby brother. Delilah was a tall, sturdy girl with chin-length wavy hair and shining dark eyes. Her mom was a petite darker version of her. Delilah exuded confidence. She made excellent eye contact, read like a dream, and gave serious thought before she gave long definitions for the vocabulary portion of the test.

Mom told me frankly, as the baby squirmed uncontrollably in her arms, that the baby was deaf and blind. He had just learned to crawl even though he was over a year old. I was a little stunned by this information. My six-month-old grandson had just started crawling and I sent up a silent thought of gratitude for a healthy child.

Delilah turned out to be bossy, ADHD, and headstrong. She had a temper and wasn't afraid of anyone. That temper frequently got her in trouble. Our assistant principal made many calls home to her mom about fights on the playground.

A great teacher learns something from every single student. Some students, however, are better teachers than others. Delilah became one of my best teachers. In fact, she taught me two important lessons.

Delilah's baby brother was hard to manage. She frequently had claw marks on her face and arms from his scratching. He was always fighting and squirming in his mother's arms. He often had to travel out of state for surgeries. I felt extremely sorry for the mom to have the battle of taking care of the demands of such a tough situation. I also admired her straightforwardness, her understanding of her difficult 7-year-old, and her practicality.

Delilah loved her brother as fiercely as a mother tiger. She once wrote a story in writer's workshop about her night at home. It was so startling and it changed me. She wrote about how the baby fought during dinner and spit his food everywhere and how Delilah just laughed and cleaned it up. After dinner, they had a tickling fight until they couldn't breathe. At bath time, the baby peed everywhere. They all thought it was hilarious. Then Delilah kissed her brother goodnight. She finished her story with, "I love my brother."

It made it apparent to me that all children can be joyous and can be a joy. Their home was still a home full of love and laughter regardless of the struggles they had in their world.

That was early in the year. The other life-changing lesson Delilah taught me came halfway through the year. Exactly.

In kindergarten and first grade, classes celebrate the 100th day of school. It is because they are learning to count to 100. I feel that second graders should have a tougher concept. So we had a "Half Way Through Second Grade" party. Shortly before that day,

I sent the class to their seats with the problem of figuring out which day would be half way through the year. They had to find what was half of 170 or 180. (The number of days per year varied depending on the teachers' contract.) It was a very tough problem for them. Most years someone came up with the solution somewhat accidentally. When we figured out which number day it was, we scheduled a little party.

At the "Half Way Through Second Grade" celebration, everyone got a half doughnut with their lunch. The class was always boisterous and noisy because of the treat. The year Delilah was there we had meatballs for lunch. Cara, the aide for my autistic student, helped pass out the doughnuts. Cara was seven months pregnant and waddled back to our table. She and I sat down to eat our lunches.

Suddenly, Delilah came running toward me, holding her throat. My first thought was she was about to throw up, and then I realized she was choking. Without even thinking I hurried behind her and ordered, "Raise your arms and cough!" She just gave me a panicked look. I wrapped my arms around her and thought, "Okay, let's see if I know how to do this." I squeezed. Delilah was only a few inches shorter than I am and weighed close to 90 pounds. She tightened her stomach and pulled me down to the floor. "Cara, help me!"

Cara knew with her seven-month baby bump there was no way she could wrap her arms around Delilah. Instead, she ran and buzzed the office then hurried out of the room to get help. I tried again. Delilah took me down again.

I knew Sonia, the teacher next door, knew how to do a Heimlich so I ran for her. Delilah came running out after me. Sonia wasn't there. Delilah was trying to drink water in the hall drinking fountain. Since she couldn't swallow, water just ran down her face. I grabbed her again and squeezed. Still she was holding herself as tight as a pole. She was fighting me like a drowning person.

Just as she pulled me down again full throttle, the nurse, Cara and the assistant principal came sprinting down the hall toward us. The nurse shouted, "Can she cough?" Either the force

of the fall or the suggestion of a cough had dislodged what was

stuck. A meatball popped out of Delilah's mouth.

Delilah started crying. "Can I call my mommy?"

Cara stood next to us, puffing from all the running. She

held emergency forms with the phone numbers on it and calmly

said, "I'm doing it right now, honey."

I got up off the floor. Delilah and I were both covered in

vomit. We stumbled to the bathroom to clean ourselves off. I was

trembling and fighting tears. Cara came back and said she would

cover the class while I went down stairs with the nurse and

Delilah.

A few minutes later, Delilah's mom came rushing in. "She

scared me to death," I whispered to her.

Her mom replied, "Somehow, I knew when I saw the

school number on my phone, she wasn't just in trouble again."

Just then, Delilah popped out of the nurse's office and ran

straight into her mother's arms. Mom looked her up and down

and said, "Well, I guess we won't have meatballs tonight. I do hope Ms. Meredith chastised you and reminded you to chew your food." We all laughed, albeit shakily.

As they left school, I looked at the assistant principal. "I'll be sore tomorrow. She fought me for all she was worth. And I just learned a life lesson. You can't save someone's life unless they'll let you."

There are two mini sequels to this story. First, one of the rabbits in my hat to get the class to quiet down was to start the beginning of a phrase and the class would finish it. For example, if I called "Macaroni and...." The class responded with, "Cheese!" Or "George..." "Washington!" The most popular one was always "Spaghetti and...." "Meatballs!" It took a long time to get everyone not to turn and look at Delilah after the meatball incident.

The other story took place the following Christmas. My now-grown kids, my mother, a family friend, and I were having a quiet day. At Christmas dinner, my mom choked on her food. She began to turn fuchsia. We all jumped out of our chairs. My adult

children looked panicked. Tom grabbed his phone wondering if

he should call 911. As I wrapped my arms around Mom, I thought,

"Well, I guess I'll find out if I do know how to do this after all." I

squeezed. Out shot the chicken she was choking on. That time I

really was a hero. Being my mother, she simply sat back down

and finished eating. Not a thank you, not a "Gee, you save my

life." Not a "Wow, I really needed that." What I now know is I do

know how to do a Heimlich. I just don't ever want to have to do it

again.

CHAPTER 12

WHAT MY HEART HEARD

I shake everyone's hand as they enter the room in the morning. "Good morning, Wesley. Good morning, Kenny. Good morning, Mary Beth. Good morning, Amy. Are you okay? I'll talk to you in just a sec. Put your stuff away and I'll be right in. Good morning, Susie. Good morning, Daryl. A gentleman takes his hat off in the building. No, huh? A new haircut? Okay."

I walked in the room and called Daryl over. "Who is one person who you trust? Glenn? Good. A girl? Shannon? Shannon, will you take Daryl in the corner back there. He has a new haircut and is worried about it."

Shannon is a nice girl. I'd never send a "mean girl" for this job. I hear her whisper from the corner behind my desk. "Oh, the front is great! Can I look at the back?"

I asked Glenn to give an opinion also. "Dude, I wish my mom would let me get that haircut. She tells me if I'm good, I can get a fauxhawk."

Meanwhile, I sat Amy next to me but did not look at her. With some kids you can have a private conversation eye to eye but not with Amy. "What's going on?"

While I had my conversation with Amy, I took attendance, filled out the lunch forms, and collected field trip money.

Big snuffle. "Nothin'"

"But you're crying." She took a shuddering breath.

I waited. Some kids will let you use humor to loosen them up. Not Amy.

She took a deep shaky breath. "My mommy told me I was grounded."

"Oh, nuts! Why?"

"'Cuz I dropped my drink in the car."

"Oh, what a mess! I bet she was frustrated. Was it on the way to school?"

"Yeah. I took the lid off and we stopped real fast."

"What can I do to help you not worry about it all day? How will you fix it after school?"

"I can help her clean the car maybe. She will probably do it now though."

"How about writing her a note?"

"Oh, okay." She brightened.

"You can use some special paper if you want. Will you show it to me when you've finished?"

Daryl had amassed some haircut admirers. He had put his hat away and was sitting on the rug with his friends, chatting and laughing.

Kids live in the real world. Their worries don't stop at the classroom door. They love their families more than anyone else. If mom is cross, it worries them. If dad is mad about his damn car, teachers hear about it frequently with the "D" word whispered. If the parents' friend dies suddenly, the child suffers, too.

Daryl and Amy's problems were easy to fix. Bigger problems are not so easy. Sometimes their lives are just a mess or they've had an unspeakable tragedy.

I had a child whose parents were killed in a murder-suicide. Dakota was just a baby and she has had the best kind of parenting since then. She knew her parents were dead, but she had no real memory of them. She did not seem to have any memory of the incident. Dakota did relate very well with another orphan, Harry Potter.

Sometimes the child remembers the tragedy. Bridget was the oldest child of five. She was the oldest girl and in a Latin household that meant she was the little mother. Her mom was in the other room dressing the baby. Bridget was helping her two-year-old sister find the sister's missing jacket when a terrible accident occurred and the little sister was killed. I have never been quite sure what happened. Bridget was a little-bitty six-year-old when it happened, but she blamed herself. Of course,

the family services investigated and determined it was an

accident. Afterward, the family moved out of state to Chicago to

escape the small town gossip.

In first grade, all Bridget could do was talk about her sister

dying. By the time second grade came, she wouldn't mention her

sister's name. She was bright, beautiful, and completely closed

off. I asked if she wanted to talk about it. She just stared at me.

"Sweetheart, I will be ready to listen when you are ready

to talk," I told her. I talked to the school social worker, who told

me if she wasn't talking about it she was probably fine. I

immediately got our outside counselor, Terri Treman, to reach

out to Bridget and her family. Mom was very sad, worried, and

feeling hugely guilty.

I had a program in the room that year from Ravinia Music

Festival, a prestigious summer music venue. The artist, Michael

Miles, came to our room for the first time in November. Many of

the children knew Michael from the prior year and were wildly acting as if a rock star had just entered the class. Bridget held back from participating. The class stood in a circle and we all sang *Rocking Robin* together. The kids bopped around the room happily. Then Michael said, "I'm going to play a song that is just guitar, no singing. I want you to listen, and then we will talk about how the music made you feel."

I watched the class as they sat on the rug next to their friends. Some shut their eyes, some swayed back and forth, some diddled around. Bridget put her head down to her chest. I moved next to her and put my arm around her. She wrapped her arms around me and began to sob. She sobbed and sobbed and sobbed.

"I know how you feel, Bridget. My husband died. It's so hard to miss someone, isn't it?" She nodded. I just kept quietly murmuring to her, trying to keep myself from starting to cry, also.

Michael looked a little stunned but talked to the class until I was able to untangle myself from a spent little girl. I sent her for a drink of water in the hall. She wandered out, taking huge

shuddering breaths.

After that, Bridget would talk about that poor lost baby.

She asked if she could put the little sister's picture on her desk.

She became more open, made friends, smiled, and laughed. The

family eventually moved back to the town they had come from.

The grief counseling at Children's' Memorial Hospital helped the

family move forward.

At the end of the year, Bridget wrote a thank you note to

Michael.

Dear Michael,

Thank you for making me remember my sister. It made me happy.

Love,

Bridget

Some children's lives, like Bridget's, are sad, but there is

hope. It's very rare that I encountered a child whose life was such

a mess I had very little hope to help resolve their problems.

However, some of these kids had lives that made my skin crawl and gave me nightmares.

The Exorcist is the first thing I think of when I hear the word "Devil." I want to be an exorcist. I didn't back in the day. That movie freaked me out. I slept with the lights on for over a year.

I've met a few devils. I don't know if I believe they are evil. I do believe that their pain causes them to objectify the people around them. Perhaps they were objects first.

I think about Josiah. He was probably being sexually abused. He was screaming for help. His ADHD meant he couldn't control his skewed impulses. Josiah groped both boys and girls. He had this truly nasty thing he did where he would put his forearm across the inside of a classmate's wrist when it was lying upwards on a desk. He would actually take their hand and flip the arm so the soft side was upwards. He then laid his arm across their arm and put all his body weight on it. I'd never seen anyone do that before. It always produced a loud yelp and tears. Try it. It hurts like bloody hell and doesn't leave any marks. "What?" he would declare. "I didn't mean to hurt him. It was an accident."

He drew graphic pictures of penises. He used words like "boner." He talked about girls' juicy butts. Feces were smeared on bathroom walls. The Department of Children and Family Services wouldn't take my complaint that he was being abused. He hadn't told me and I couldn't see any signs of physical abuse. Being psychic wasn't enough, I guess. They suggested he might be watching something inappropriate on television. They would have taken the complaint if he was five, but he was already eight.

His father avoided me. He did not come to meetings. When he did, the special education team surrounded me for fear my straight shooting would make things worse. The charms I had put on my room to keep evil out seemed to work. He only came in once early in the year. He wouldn't look me in the eye when we did meet.

After I made the call to DCFS, I took Josiah into an office with another teacher. These conferences should never happen without a witness.

"You know I know when you are lying, right?" He broadcast lies to me like NBC. "I told the class when kids say or do things that are only for adults, it can be a sign that an adult is doing that to them. Do you remember when I said that?"

He nodded.

"Are you seeing these things in a movie or on television?"

He shook his head.

"Is someone doing them to you?"

He glanced up at me. "N-n-n...." As he looked me in the eye, he stopped and hung his head again.

I wanted to vomit. "Do you trust me?" He nodded. "You can tell me." He just shook his head.

The other teacher looked as nauseous as I felt. "You know you can trust Ms. Meredith. You can tell her if you need to."

We sat in silence for a while. He said nothing. He never did.

Yes, I've met the devil and I do want to be an exorcist.

CHAPTER 13

KEEP COOL!

Russian Proverb: Patience doesn't always help, but impatience

never does.

One day during a math lesson, my student teacher, Jane,

was teaching the class. I was doing an observation on another

student. I heard, "Victory!" shouted by my best friend Nelson. He

was lying on his back, arms and legs in the air.

"Nelson! Come here," I demanded. He came and stood in

front of me with a hound dog look on his face. "Did you just shout

victory?"

There was a long pause. His eyes rolled left to right, as if

he was trying to rewind to two minutes earlier. "Yes." He sounded chagrined, although I was uncertain if it was due to being in trouble or being interrupted in his fantasy.

"Why?" Mostly, I asked out of curiosity. I just wondered in which of many possible battles he had just reigned supreme in his mind.

His shoulders shrugged. I shook my head. "Do you suppose you could do a couple more math problems before you return to the battle?"

He smiled sheepishly. "I'll try."

I don't perceive myself as a patient person, but I am often told how patient I am. I sometimes wonder why that is. Perhaps it is the moment or more likely the situation.

I am not patient with long-winded meetings when I have a bajillion things to do. I am not patient with drivers in front of me at tollbooths. I am not always patient in line. Probably that is when I am the least patient of all, when I am waiting in line on the phone. "All our operators are busy. You are caller number 68.

Your wait time is 2 years, 3 months, 6 days, 14 hours and 27

minutes." I always yell mean things at those recordings.

I am patient with a child who doesn't understand

something. I am wildly impatient with myself for not being able

to find a way to make it clear for them.

I am patient with the wigglers. In fact, I kind of adore

wigglers. They are so spontaneous. I frequently wonder if these

children, ADHD diagnosis or not, are in truth faeries caught in

human children's bodies, struggling to get free. They lack the

ability to put on a filter so they blurt the most outlandish things. I

do get frustrated with them. I once told my wiggly, noisy Calvin it

was a lucky thing I was single because my husband would have

wondered why I said, "Calvin, Calvin, Calvin," over and over in my

sleep. I once counted how often I said Calvin's name in a half hour

during class: 29 times.

I know self-restraint isn't part of these kids' skill set, but I

did want them, at the very least, to try. Sometimes the "try" is

almost as funny as the blurt. I once filled a full page of notebook paper, front and back, writing as fast as I could in an attempt to record every movement Nelson made in a half an hour. I'd start to write and look up: Nelson was somewhere across the room. This happened each time I'd look down. Up to sharpen his pencil, back to his desk, do a math problem, visit a friend across the room, break his pencil on purpose, scoot back to his desk, get up to sharpen the pencil again. Over and over. He did manage to get a little work done. Not much, mind you.

What exactly would impatience do? It would make Nelson or any other child feel rotten about himself—something that just happened because Nelson had no, not any, self-control. It wouldn't help him accomplish anything. It would not teach him self-restraint. In fact, it would probably be worse.

I have a myriad of gimmicks for these kids. For Nelson, none of them seemed to work. The air cushion I gave him to sit on became a rolling wobbly thing to toss, a resistance band to kick on the base of his chair became something to trample into the ground, and stress balls became missiles in the air. I just took a lot of deep breaths and tried to see the humor in it. Even sitting in a

chair rather than on the rug didn't help. He'd fall off the chair at

least once a day. Each time he looked so startled, I had to try not

to laugh.

One thing that just causes my patience to evaporate is

heat. I can be patient and redirect the worst behavior until the

thermometer in my room hits tropical. I don't know what causes

me to become a raving maniac. Maybe I have a lower-than-

average body temperature. Maybe my northern European blood

can't process it.

My only brother, Adam, lives in Queens. He called me on

one hot, sultry day. There was a power outage in New York City.

"It's broiling," he complained. "You know how we Schutz girls

are." We both laughed. That Schutz girls or boys don't suffer the

heat well is a bit of an understatement. We get crabby and

sometimes just plain mean.

My classroom never had air conditioning. The first couple

of years only a few rooms in our 1920-something school did. Each year, a few more rooms were added to the Land of Cool. Finally,

about five years ago, there were only four classrooms left. Room

203 was one of those rooms. The new engineer said we could not

get any more units. The city would not allow it. It had something

to do with airflow.

We faced east. With the longer, late spring days, the room

was usually 80 degrees when I arrived in the morning in late May

and early June. Both ceiling and box fans would go on. As there is

rarely an easterly wind in Chicago, windows would stay closed

with the shades drawn. No sunlight was allowed to enter. The

lights were off. The goal was to keep it from getting any hotter.

After several years of experimentation, I knew these were the

best options.

I kept a spray bottle of water in my mini refrigerator to

squirt our faces and the inside of our arms. I taught the class then

to blow on the inside of their wrists. Natural air conditioning, I'd

tell them. I gave lots of drinking fountain breaks.

We did low-key work. Who can learn in that environment? Studies show 72 degrees is the optimal learning temperature. By 10 a.m., my room was well into the 80s. Studies also show behavior deteriorates in the heat. My deterioration was the worst in the room. My temper fuse was about a quarter inch long. I took lots of deep breaths to keep it there.

There were always two or three students who, like me, just couldn't handle the heat. They alternated between pacing the room like a caged lion at the zoo and wilting over their desk like a wet rag. These students were usually my Nelsons or Calvins.

We tried everything to keep learning going. Other teachers would offer their classrooms when their kids were at library or fine arts. We would join other classes to eat our lunch in the relative cool. When my co-workers complained about the noise the air conditioners made, I just stared at them.

So in the dark days of June, we created beautiful things. We studied the solar system in our dark room. We made craters in powdered tempera paint mixed with flour by dropping rocks into the "moon dust." We created our own constellations with cereal boxes and wrote myths to tell the corresponding stories.

Each June, we would do an author study of Eve Bunting. Partners would select a book at their level and create projects to show off the story. Dioramas, posters, interviews with characters, songs telling the story or dozens of other ideas filled the darkened room. We damply listened to each other as each child read a favorite part of his book to the class.

We did poetry slams. On Monday, each student selected a poem to be read in the slam on Friday. We practiced each day. We had done this all year, but second grade was coming to an end and students searched for the "perfect" poem.

On hot, stuffy Friday mornings, we'd sit in a circle on the rug. Poems lay on the floor in front of our laps. I'd pick a stick with a student's name to start. In her or his best voice, they read with inflection and expression. Reading was paced carefully for effect. After each poem, we'd snap our fingers, coffee house style. Then the person on the left of the reader would begin. Jack Prelutsky poems made us laugh. Mattie Stepanek's poems made us sigh

and tear up. It was simply beautiful, heartfelt reading and

listening.

And for a few precious moments we were remarkably

cool.

CHAPTER 14

THE DILEMMA OF EMPATHY

October meant taffy apple sales. Oh yum! Nearly everyone wanted to bite into sweet crunchy slightly tart apple covered with caramel. It makes me smack my lips just thinking about it.

I have in my mind's eye that impulsive child (usually a boy, but my Eleanor was one too) who had scored a taffy apple for lunch. Their moms had lovingly put one in their bookbag to eat later. Control, however, wasn't theirs. So they came up the stairs before school started and lined up at the classroom door. Eyes twinkled on the caramelized faces. Their hands were sticky and their tongues crept out of their mouths, licking their lips as far as

the tongue could reach.

"Good morning, Kenny. Your mom packed you a taffy

apple for lunch?"

Kenny, or Ellie, or Humberto looked down and then

peeked up. "Um....I just wanted to taste it."

It was so hard not to laugh. I completely sympathized.

"Was it tasty?"

They would nod earnestly, relieved I understood. "I love

taffy apples, too. Ian, can you take Kenny to the bathroom? He

needs to remove his sugar coating."

I am chock full of empathy. I am wildly intuitive. I see

things others don't see and know things that I have no idea how I

know. I don't mean jumping to conclusions, although I do that

sometimes. I just understand things. I could see when the kids

were lying. It became so pronounced that I eventually saw the lies

in waves of light pouring off their heads like Medusa's snake hair.

I would jokingly tell the class I was psychic. Inevitably, they would ask, "What am I thinking?"

"You're thinking you can trick me," I'd counter. I never knew how to explain that I wasn't a mind reader.

My wild connection with children this age was that I remembered very clearly what it was to be seven and eight. I was the oldest child with five younger siblings. Even as a child, I was known to be the one who could talk to anyone and make them feel comfortable. Still, how did I know that Abner didn't mean to hit someone with the ball? He was just too excited when he threw it. The assistant principal once called me the lie whisperer. I joked that the angels whispered the truth in my ear. I don't know how I knew the truth, but it happened daily.

I wasn't as great with my own kids after Mark died. We muddled through. Elena was brutally honest. Oh, sure, she'd sneak behind my back to do things. Then she left the evidence lying around with the intention of getting caught. Still, her choices were mostly reasonable. There were no huge problems.

She had a strong self-protection mechanism that kept her out of the worst of it. She wanted to be happy and tried hard to be in that place.

Tom, my wildly brilliant, deep thinking, once happy boy, on the other hand, was lost in his despair. He started dating a wonderful girl within a couple weeks of Mark's funeral. You would have thought that would make him happier. He was happier, but only when he was with her. Together they protested the upcoming war in Iraq. I felt that was a reasonable outlet for his anger. I knew he was smoking both cigarettes and reefer. I had told him more than once I hated it. He was so very angry with the unfairness of the world that it didn't really matter what I or anyone else said. My role as his very worried protector came quickly.

A week or two after Mark's death, Tom was sitting in a classroom at Whitney Young High School, a selective enrollment Chicago public high school that was the premier high school in the state. He was a junior and had been at Whitney Young since seventh grade when he started in their gifted program. The

classroom was an interior room with no windows. He didn't much

like the teacher. For about a year, he had been writing free verse

wherever and whenever possible. I had read most of it. He would

hand it to me then walk away. It was dark but not suicidal. His dad

was dying. Of course, it was cynical and brooding.

This teacher had seen a sentence that had said something

like "I dream of death" and had turned it in to the school

psychologist. I agree that she should have done that. But as a

teacher, I felt she should have also reached out to Tom. He

wanted that teacher, or for that matter, any of his teachers, to

acknowledge his grief. Only his art teacher had given him a card

and a journal.

On that particular day, Tom had had enough. He had

found out about how this teacher had turned in his writing to the

office. He was attempting to get human contact and felt he had

been treated as a number, a weirdo, a recluse. He felt caged in

the room and knew he was about to lose his tenuous hold of his temper. He got up and left the room. He went to the cafeteria

and sat with friends.

I got a call from school. This was the first I had heard of

the "I dream of dying" writing. "Did anyone talk to him about it?"

I ask. No. He would have to serve detention on March 20. "This is

ridiculous," I told them. "His dad just died. Is this how you help

someone who is grieving?"

When I talked to Tom about it, my first question was, "Are

you wanting to die? Are you thinking of killing yourself?"

"No." He actually curled his lip at this question.

"Why did you write it?" I knew what he was going to tell

me.

"Dad died right here, Mom." He waved his arm around our

now put-back-to-normal living room. "In pain! That was so

fucking unfair!" I want to wrap my arms around him and cry, but

we were not in that mode in those days. He held me at arm's

length most of the time. He was angry with me, also, for not

saving his dad. He was angry at himself for feeling that way. I knew it and it broke my heart. My sweet boy, the boy who had been a delightful child, easygoing and friendly, was lost in his despair. I felt like I was losing him as certain as I had lost his father.

I talked to the counselor on the phone. "His dad just died. Isn't there a way to allow him to get out of a class without counting it as a cut and giving him a detention?" She told me it would require a 504, an accommodation for his learning. It would require Tom seeing a social worker outside of school, on my bill, three times to confirm he needed it.

I frantically began the search for a mental health practitioner. The only one I could find who took teens, was covered by my medical plan, and was available ASAP was a woman in her late 50s. She was a grief specialist, I was told. It was apparent after the first session, she and Tom were not well suited. "Only two more visits, Tom. We can do this." I was rushing him through this so we could get his accommodation, which I knew he needed desperately.

Tom's 17th birthday was March 19. Elena, the girlfriend, and I took Tom to an Irish pub for dinner. We were having a pleasant meal and enjoying ourselves together, which was a rare treat. Someone walked in the room and announced that the invasion of Iraq had started and we were at war. The enjoyable evening was ended abruptly. Fear, frustration, and anger replaced the fun in a blink of an eye.

The next day students all over Chicago were leaving school and going downtown to protest the war. Whitney Young had forbidden their students from exiting the building but let them have a sit-in in the cafeteria. That was where Tom's friends and girlfriend were when he got up and walked out on his detention.

His walking out of detention, a stupid unwarranted detention in my mind, brought a three-day suspension. He would get to pick his suspension dates, I was told. Being no dummy, Tom picked them to coincide with a three-day weekend. This is crazy, I thought. He got a six days weekend! The whole thing felt nuts.

Tom had his final meeting with the social worker. He climbed in the car afterwards, fuming. He ranted about how all she did was lecture him and never listened to him. Later that day, I got a call from her. She said she would write the letter recommending his accommodation. She said Tom was very angry. Well, duh! She also told me I needed to take a stand on allowing Tom to smoke marijuana. I told her to shove off. She thought I was wrong. I told her the time to break habits is not when you are in the middle of grief. I asked her if she would have recommended an adult stop drinking at this point in their lives? She admitted she would not. After I hung up, I wondered if she was even ethically supposed to tell me about Tom's drug use as it was not life threatening.

I was grateful to her only in that I now had someone to be pissed off at. My mother always told me: *I may not agree with you and you'll know it. But I will defend your right to do it to the end.* That was how I felt that day.

We did get an accommodation for Tom. He could leave class if he needed to. He was told he could go visit the school psychologist or the attendance officer if he left class. He would have an appointment with the psychologist weekly. The counselor then said, "No more cuts." I asked her to check his records for any cuts prior to the one he had detention for. There were none. Next she added, "No more leaving school." I pointed out even when he cut and when he left his detention, he hadn't left school. After the counselor went lecture someone else, the school psychologist leaned over and asked Tom, "You left detention for the anti-war sit in?"

"Yes, ma'am."

"Good! A little protest is good for the soul." She winked at him. "Just don't tell them I said that." *Thank you, thank you, and thank you.*

Tom gave me a lot of grief for several years. In fairness, I know he really didn't want to do that. He was just stuck in this terrible emotional place. I rarely told anyone of my worry for him. Mostly, he was wildly angry and depressed. It manifested itself in some astonishingly creative swearing. I can't even write some of the things he said. I'm not sure if he talked that way to everyone or if he saved it for me. It was never directed at me but "stupid" people he encountered or politicians. He just liked to vent. Perhaps "spew" is a better word. I would let it go until it became too vile or violent, and then I'd tell him I couldn't listen anymore. He would take a deep breath, then sheepishly say, "Sorry, Mom."

Except for when he and his girlfriend broke up, the night before he was to start community college, I didn't worry about suicide. That micro-burst passed relatively quickly. After the negative experience with the social worker, he wasn't interested in counseling. He just wasted time and money partying with his friends. The same friends he had for years with an occasional new one in the mix. They spent a lot of time at my house and only one boy rang my finely-tuned alarm bell, but that was because this

boy was a leach not a leader. Mostly, they were great kids who

watched out for my son and made me laugh at their antics.

Back in my classroom, I taught kids to become fluent

readers, I read hundreds of books to them, and I read their minds

as well. It helped me climb out of the rubble of my life back to the

sweet and slightly tangy joy of living.

CHAPTER 15

STYLING

My classroom had several hats hanging on the walls. There was a black one, a cream straw one with flowers, a turquoise straw pillbox with a fascinator, and a brown one with bright pink flowers. Eventually, I had nine hats. My favorite was a fuchsia feathered pillbox that had once belonged to Mark's grandmother Alice.

I once attended a workshop where the presenter had a strategy for stopping interruptions while teaching. She wore a piece of cardboard on a string around her neck. One side was colored red. The other side was colored green. When the green side was out, the students were free to talk to her. When the red was out, they had to let her work with someone else without interrupting her. The intention was to let her work with a group without being bombarded with questions, problems, or squabbles.

This seemed like a reasonable plan, mostly. I'm not a fancy person but I do take time selecting my clothing. Everything has to match: pants, shirt, socks, shoes, coat, jewelry, and ideally, even my underwear. (It's just hard to do that perfectly.) I was simply not going to wear a piece of cardboard on a string around my neck.

Instead, I used old hats. I started with four or five I bought on eBay in a vintage lot and built from there. I'd find a black one I liked better than the one in the room and I'd replace it. People gave me fantastic hats and it was a blast using them.

During the tai chi phase of second grade, I would ask the students what they thought the hats were for and why there were so many colors. They had lots of ideas. They'd guess for storytelling, for yelling or maybe as a sign to get quiet. I explained that when I was wearing a hat, they were not allowed to interrupt me. I might be working with a group or having a private conversation with a classmate. They were only allowed interrupt me if someone was vomiting or bleeding. Period!

I next had them ponder the reason for so many colors: days of the week, a different one for each reading group, or one for each subject. Usually a girl, but sometimes a fashion savvy boy, would hit upon the need for the hat to match my outfit. Why should I wear black with navy? Let's be real here.

I wore the hats often. Students would come up while I was working with someone and I would glance at them, point at my hat, and pointedly ignore them. Inevitably, they would groan or sigh and walk away and solve their own problem. They knew how to do whatever task I had left them to do. They understood I was giving a classmate or a group of classmates my undivided attention.

Having style doesn't have to be a hat. Being short and entirely too round, I wasn't going to take up high fashion. So hats

were the physical style of my room. I had lots of personality and
teaching style also. My true style showed in how I acted and
reacted.

In fact, for a while after Mark's death, the classroom was
the only place I had any style a.k.a. confidence. I once read your
spouse is your mirror. They reflect who you are to the world. Your
partner helps measure what is too little or too much of your
behavior.

When Mark died, my mirror shattered. I was left with
shards of varying sizes, some long and narrow, some teeny tiny.
The edges were sharp. I bled as I tried to lift them to glimpse who
I was. It was so confusing. Some shards held certain images—the
parent image for example. That shard was missing the other cop,
good or bad, to balance my parenting. How could I be tough or
easy without my counterweight?

I never expected some of the broken reflections. Some
seemed to be part of a memory of myself. I questioned the
images: "Hello, is that you in there?"

The only piece of the mirror where the reflection remained full sized and undamaged was my teacher image. Perhaps that was due to the fact that I had only been teaching three years when he died. Perhaps it was due to my teaching life being mine alone, never really belonging to Mark's influences. Probably it was a little of each. I was confident in the classroom even in the early days after returning from Mark's funeral. I was able to use my passion to fill in my voids and to begin refurbishing my mirror.

Most years, I had at least one student teacher. It is a joy of teaching in Chicago that student teachers abound, if your school has been noticed by education programs. We had dozens of student teachers each year. I primarily worked with The Erikson Institute, which specializes in early childhood education, and their students spend a year in the classroom. I also had students from National Lewis, North Park, Northeastern, Northwestern, Loyola, Roosevelt and DePaul universities. Most of these women and men were awesome.

Being a teacher of teachers gave me tremendous joy and made me reflect on my classroom practices. I tried to give my student teachers just enough support. Our school was a great place to student-teach because we were a creative bunch of teachers who tried to stay in the forefront of education. It gave the learning teachers a chance to try new things. It also might have been a terrible place to student-teach as they would have a hard time finding a school as accommodating to individual teachers.

If you haven't read *If I Ran the Circus* by Dr. Seuss recently, you should. The main character plans an outrageous circus. His job appears to be planning and being the ringmaster, while his friend, Mr. Sneelock, does all the daring dirty work. The story culminates with Sneelock diving from an absurd height into a tiny glass of water. I often joked that book is what teaching is about. A good student teacher is like the sidekick character, Mr. Sneelock. If you do it right, they will even dive into a glass of water if needed. Not that I expected that level of blind devotion or selflessness. In fact, being a teacher is very much like being

Sneelock and it was good practice for them. It's interesting what

my student teachers recall about being in Room 203.

Jane had been with me part-time in the fall of the year

with my most difficult class, the group I called my Whac-a-Mole

class. I almost fell on my knees to thank her when she asked if she

could do her full-time student teaching in the spring. She saved

me. That group required as many adults as possible. Even five or

six teachers couldn't hold them in check long.

Jane remembers Nelson lying on the floor, spinning on his

side. She was impressed by my patience with him. What I

remember about that was if I let Nelson spin on the floor he

actually listened to what was going on in the room. If I tried to

make him sit still, he couldn't hear me because he was so focused

on just sitting still. He was the dust mop of the room. Did it make

me nuts? You bet! That, however, was my problem, not his.

Ryan, my wonderful 6' 6" student teacher, thinks of a

slippery skirt. It was a very nice, stylish, in fact, dark red peasant skirt. I looked good. Ryan and I were sitting on the hard, smooth,

dark blue second grade chairs watching the class present

projects. I bent forward to pick something up off the floor. As I

leaned forward, the chair went backwards. I could feel it

happening. Slowly but steadily the chair slid until with a loud

bump, I was on the floor. The boys fell over laughing. The girls

hopped up to rescue me. I was a little rattled, but I picked myself

up and we went back to work.

Ryan says that memory reminds him when he messes up

as a teacher to just relax and take everything in stride. (By the

way, the Salvation Army got a very nice skirt the next weekend.)

Frank DeJohns was my first student teacher. He later

became a co-worker and for many years has been a good friend.

Frank left a job at an advertising agency and knew he wanted to

teach. He had very little experience with kids or at least

classroom experience before he started in our room. His first

assigned task was to teach phonics. Frank held onto that

teacher's manual like it was Moses' tablets. After one lesson, when the most well-behaved children were crawling around,

Frank was very understandably frustrated. At that point, I wanted

to take the damn teacher's manual and toss it out the window. I

convinced him to modify the lesson, which he did grudgingly. It's

hard to imagine Frank starting like that because he is now a

remarkably innovative teacher with fantastic classroom

management.

Frank also came to class dressed as Christopher Columbus

on Columbus Day. The kids thought it was hysterical and

reminded him of it for years. He says, "You taught me to go all

out and teach kids that it's okay to make a complete ass of

yourself as long as it gets the desired results."

My last student teacher was Jessica Petertil. I felt as if the

Universe gave her to me wrapped in hand stamped paper and

tied a cloth bow. Our class was full of super bright monkeys who

certainly had naughty tendencies.

"I remember the little 'line of complaints' that would form

during lunch time at the back table," she said. "They were ready and wanting to bring it all to you and you were ready to hear it in some way or another. Your face would quickly and genuinely change from talking with one student, who maybe had a sensitive friendship situation going on or a hard day, to then the next issue, maybe of a complaint of some type of ridiculous sexual comment being made at the table."

Ah, yes! The ridiculous sexual comment. That group could creatively shock all of us with the things they said. They weren't particularly knowledgeable, but they loved to make each other gasp with their naughtiness.

One day, Jessica was teaching a lesson while I was outside in the hall testing students. There was a substitute in the room with her helping to maintain order. Sergio, my fashionista, and Elmer were attempting to rattle other student, Amelia. Amelia was a rock solid, down-to- earth, cowboy boot wearing pragmatist. She was hard to rattle, so they had to bring in the truly startling phrase. "Nipples," Sergio whispered to her.

Elmer lost it. "Nipple! Nipple! Nipple!"

Sergio had to throw in a few more "nipple" taunts. Amelia rolled her eyes and ignored them. Mr. Dirty Words in the Unabridged Dictionary, Joel, leaned in for the kill. "You're a nipplemaster!" Sergio and Elmer fell over laughing as Amelia told them they could not talk to her that way.

At this point, Jessica sent the boys to the thinking chair to settle down. She was unaware of what they had been saying but knew that they weren't on task. Amelia didn't tattle, so no one was abreast of what had happened.

Fast forward to lunch. The complaint line had formed as I was trying to get two consecutive bites of my sandwich. Next up was Bingo. He was one of my students who couldn't pronounce their Rs. "Ms. Mewedif! Joel said somefing totawy innapwopweate to Ewmo!"

I called Elmer and Joel over and asked Elmer what Joel had said to him. He covered his face with his hands and mumbled, "He called me nipplemaster. He said it to Amelia first." My mouth dropped open. The aide for one of my students was sitting next to me. She gasped and started to choke on her salad.

Jessica pounded her on the back while trying not to laugh.

"You said *what*? Good grief, where did you hear that?

Your grandma is *so* going to have a cow when I tell her." Then I

called out, "Will someone buzz the office?" I requested a visit

from the principal.

I wasted an hour of my time trying to sort what had

occurred. This included a conference with the Principal Zelenka

and the boys. I explained these boys had invented a new

compound word. Not surprisingly, no one wanted to tell the

principal what that word was. We finally learned that adding

"master" to the end of any word simply made it more shocking.

Those boys taught all of us something we didn't particularly want

to learn. It also gave us something to laugh about after school.

There was a lesson about that beautiful balance between

frustration and joy.

Have you ever noticed that the quietest people say the

most profound things when they finally open their mouths to

speak? My quietest sidekick, Erin, summed up my goal as a supervising teacher and brought home the whole point of the thing.

"I think what I learned most in your classroom . . . is not really a trick per se, but that teaching is essentially joyful work," she said. "And that, taking the time to laugh— when Paval tells you that he dreams in French or the Unhappy Genius draws a mustache on his face instead of completing his writing—is sustaining. It sustains you not just during the ups and downs that inevitably come in the course of the classroom year, but in your own life as well."

I had forgotten about the mustache. The memory of the twirly black marker mustache under his smeary glasses made me laugh for days. The spirals were so dense that if he could have stretched that mustache out it would have been three feet long. It was a shame to make him wash it off.

Each student teacher was different. My job was to find

what their strengths were and polish those while building up

what they were lacking. I had high expectations, but I was also

relaxed. I know these young teachers—nearly all were young

enough to be my child—didn't always agree with me. That was

fine. In fact, that was great. It gave them a minute to try their

better way. I let them. Sometimes it worked, sometimes it didn't.

They taught me new lessons and new concepts. I dropped them

into the lion's den, pulled them out slightly chewed, patched their

wounds, gave advice on how to keep the lions at bay, and

dropped them right back in. Day after day. Most of them were

ready to tame their own lions when they left. Most of them are

still taming lions. Most of them still have a trick or two of mine

that they pull out of their sleeves when the occasion calls for it.

They are part of the sustaining joy of being a teacher.

There are several who stuck with me a whole year or a

whole life. They were my "kids" just as the seven- and eight-year-

olds were. Even better, they became precious friends. I hope I taught them to be tough, outspoken, quirky, and "stylish"

teachers. We need more of them.

CHAPTER 16

THE BEST LAID PLANS

Enrique—a wonderful, funny boy most of the time—was melting down.

He had a preliminary diagnosis of bipolar disorder. He was under a table building a sword with math snapping blocks and swearing under his breath. I was teaching the math lesson with one eye on the class and one eye on him. He charged! I was the intended victim. He slashed at me. Tricia, my student teacher, ran to the intercom and called the office.

"Yes?" queried the scratchy voice through the intercom.

"Call Enrique's mom and I need someone to take him to Ms. Zelenka," I called loudly. I didn't want to repeat the message.

Enrique lived across the street from school and his mom was usually there before the security guard. Not that day. The security guard came in as Enrique slashed at me. The blocks kept breaking off the sword and went flying across the room. He had stashed extras in his pocket. A Marine would have been impressed at how quickly he could reload.

I looked at Tricia. "There are Scholastic News magazines on the table. Do those." As the security guard carried him out over her shoulder with his arms pinned by her arms, he attempted to kick people with those crazy hard oxfords we wore. The rest of the class stared open mouthed.

I can still hear Tricia exclaiming, "Wow! This will be fun! I've never done Scholastic News with you before." Hooray for student teachers who could just go with the flow.

Someone else covered my classroom while drama enveloped the office. Enrique had kicked off his shoes and socks while his mom sat on top of him pinning his arms. He broke pottery on a shelf next to them with his bare feet. He escaped from her only to be picked up and carried to the office by a police

officer who had been called by the school clerk. The Officer

Friendly laid him on a bench and sat on him. Enrique responded

by kicking him in the groin. We tried everything to calm Enrique

down, but it ended with Enrique in a straight jacket in an

ambulance on the way to the hospital.

So much for lesson plans. They went right out the window

that day.

Lesson plans require much thought. I, like most teachers I

know, spent hours on mine. It becomes an art to put down what

the principal requires while you visualize how the lesson will

progress. When you are studying to be a teacher, the lesson plans

require every detail of what will happen—teacher's actions,

students' actions, and assessment.

I used to call those the fart lessons:

Teacher demonstrates swallowing air.

Students will swallow air.

Teacher assesses by volume of burps that follow.

Students will next fart.

Teacher assesses by the fragrance of the fart.

In reality it is practice for the real deal of teaching. You cannot just come into a room unprepared. Students can smell your unpreparedness like the farts from the above lesson.

You think about how to teach a topic, review a topic, and assess a topic. You also have to plan what to do with the smarties, the super-achievers who will be done 15 minutes before everyone else. You consider how to support the strugglers, who are behind in understanding. How do you keep all levels of your class engaged?

Just as lesson plans sometimes fly right out the window, on other days you cling to the plans as if to a life preserver.

There are days that are imprinted for eternity, our whole lives, upon our brains. Like a vignette, a tableau, they have remarkable clarity.

It was a beautiful, sunny, blue-skied Tuesday, one week into the school year. I was walking down the hall a little before 8 a.m. My student teacher that year, Frank DeJohns, came in. It was his second wedding anniversary. I greeted him with a smile. "Happy anniversary."

"Thanks," he replied distractedly. "It's weird. I just heard that a plane flew into the World Trade Center."

"What? Was it from LaGuardia? It's so close to downtown. How scary!"

How scary was right. Just as school started, whispers told us that a second plane had flown into the towers. It had to be terrorists.

Again, whispers. "The World Trade Center collapsed, imploded. It's gone." *What?* I could barely wrap my mind around it. I had stayed at the Vista Hotel in the towers with Mark as newlyweds. He had worked in the towers for Northern Trust in those days.

I had a class of 27 seven-year-olds. All day, the snatches of rumor drifted in. The Pentagon. All flights grounded, another plane headed for the White House was downed. One or two kids' families came and picked them up. Obviously, there was no recess. I wondered if I should pull my shades. We could see the Sears Tower from Room 203. Was it a target, too? Tom was in school less than a mile from there. I shoved that in the back of my mind to worry about later.

We'd whisper when other adults came in or when the class was in the hall. What was the news? We couldn't discuss it in front of the kids. It was bizarre and scary. There was a huge sense of having to be level headed and in charge. I clung to my plans that day. Anything we could do to make the abnormal feel normal helped get us through it. The flip side was we didn't want the kids to be alarmed, so routine was essential.

I gave my class the lesson about the national anthem that morning. It was an annual thing and had been planned. I can still see Frank looking at me across the rug full of children, our eyes meeting furtively. I never felt so positively American. I never felt so steadfast in my responsibility to my students. Not before, not later. Like everyone, we were stunned.

The next day, in some ways, was even stranger. I had to be prepared to discuss the events with seven-year-olds. Before school I pondered how to address it. Some kids would have been sheltered and not told about it. Others would have watched it nonstop as their parents watched. Some had parents stranded out of town. One dad was a Marine. I tried to keep it simple. It happened. We were all okay. No, I didn't know why anyone would do that.

Morning meeting was extraordinarily long on September 12th. These are not things that can be put in a lesson plan. These are the moments to teach from your heart.

CHAPTER 17

A LITTLE STRUCTURE, PLEASE

"Everyone should try to sing the national anthem," I told the class.

A little blond blue-eyed skinny boy with a voice that sounded like sixty years of cigarettes and whiskey growled, "How can we sing if we don't know the words?"

So I printed the words on flag stationery to be used in the morning. It is a ballad, a story. Early each year, I'd pass out the words and spin the story of Francis Scott Key as a prisoner on the ship at sea. I drew pictures of ramparts. We discussed seeing things in flashes of light at night—fireworks, lightning, or cameras.

They learned the song. If they didn't want to sing or if it was against their religion, I didn't force it. But they knew the words. They knew to stand straight and not talk. If they dropped something—their necklace, lunch money, or a pencil—they learned to leave it until the song was over.

"Once my cousin had tickets to the Black Hawks' game," I would tell them. "He took a few friends with him. When the national anthem played, his friends left their hats on and talked through the whole song. My cousin told me they were jerks. He said, 'I won't take them anywhere again. Not even the junkyard.'"

I tell them it's about respecting each other as well as our country. It is a life skill, I would say. Second graders love life skills.

We said the Pledge of Allegiance and sang the national anthem every morning, and I taught them to do it the correct way. Later, when they are teenagers and they decide it's a bunch of hooey, they will at least know what they are rebelling against. I hope they won't rebel against it, but I know I've done my job if they think enough about it to rebel.

Routines and clear expectations were the basis of my classroom structure. Knowing breakfast was over as soon as the pledge was done was one part of the structure. Knowing we picked sticks with people's names on them to match partners was part of the structure. Knowing if I told you to sit down now or you will have to go to the thinking chair is structure.

The tai chi beginning of every year built that structure. It is very hard for a student who transferred into our room in the middle of the year. They had to figure out the structure on their own. I usually assigned them a couple of partners to help them find their way through the maze of routines. Most second graders could manage this as they had been in school before. Once or twice we had someone who had very little school experience.

One boy named Aaron, my first year teaching, was a refugee from a war in Eastern Europe. He had been in a refugee camp in Switzerland. The family claimed he had been in school there, but it was hard to believe. He spoke his native language and German, but no English. I know about 20 words in German, most of which mean hurry up or are related to beer drinking.

Saying "Dich Ein Grosse Beir bitte" or "I'd like a large beer,

please" would not have helped much.

He hated the structure the rest of the class took for

granted. He was angry and, as is often the case with refugee kids,

very spoiled. (The parents feel guilty about the deprivation they

have faced in the past and tend to give their child whatever they

want once things settle down.) He broke every pencil and crayon

he touched, and he tore up books. He even broke markers, a feat I

didn't know was possible.

He could write his name. That was it. He didn't know his

alphabet in any language. He had no interest in reading or math

because that meant he couldn't play. He wanted to be liked by

the boys. He accomplished this by being the clown. It was

frustrating beyond belief. I tried being patient but firm. He just

yukked it up. Once when he was prancing around in the hall, I

made him stand him behind me, facing away from the class. He

simply bent over and made faces at the class from between my legs. The class would just roll their eyes at him. "Oh, Aaron!" the girls would sigh.

One day, we were hurrying to get somewhere. He tipped over his desk.

"Aaron, you'll have to clean that up when we get back! Get in line." I could hardly contain my exasperation.

He put his hands on his little boney hips and growled up at my face. "Blah, blah, blah, *blah*, blah!"

The class gasped. They stared at him with wide eyes and glanced at me to find out what I would do. And what I did was laugh. Not a wicked, "I'm going to get you now" laugh. A belly laugh. It totally disarmed him. It disarmed me, too.

"Okay. I get it. That's what I sound like to you." It reminded me of his upheaval. I'd like to tell you that was a turning point. I suppose it was a bit of one. In reality, we butted heads the rest of the year.

Around Halloween, I noticed he was beginning to speak English. We were carving pumpkins when I knew he was getting it.

"Slimy!" he yelled as he threw a handful of pumpkin innards across the room. He kicked at me as I moved him to the thinking chair.

I've always felt I let Aaron down. I wonder if the outcome would have been different if I'd gotten him my third or tenth year teaching when I had more tricks up my sleeve. As time went on, he broke fewer things and settled down a little. He never did take any interest in learning. Shortly before the year was out, the family moved out of state. I wrote to the new school recommending they have him repeat second grade. It made me never want to visit that state.

When I found myself a single mother, I was baffled by it. I still had the same idealist goal of raising happy, stable, and moderately successful (meaning they could support themselves) adults. The other cop in my good cop/bad cop teenage parenting strategy had bit the dust. I simply did not know which cop to be.

I couldn't motivate my son Tom at all. He had been this ridiculously easy child. I missed that boy. The only time he showed any motivation was to arrange an early high school graduation. This meant no early morning fights so I was relieved. Otherwise, he drove me nutty and worried me sick.

Elena hid her confusion. Her glasses were no longer rosy, but she still had a smile and a bounce most days. She worried me but no more than most mothers of teenage girls worry. In fact, her grief came to a head five or six years later while she was away at college. Then I got to be worried long distance.

Meanwhile, dinner became a crazy mess. I'd plan a meal only to have everyone disappear and I'd be eating alone. Or I'd plan to just make a sandwich because I was home alone and in would walk six hungry teenagers. I was overwhelmed by cooking and who would be eating when and where.

Just like meals, the day-to-day structure just disintegrated. Everything became a double chore. I hated paying bills because Mark and I had sat at the dining room table and worked over our finances together. Mark liked handling the little details. As a teacher, I had very little free time during the school day. After he died, I thought I had paid off a credit card. I was actually short by a dollar. The credit card company, as they are wont, charged penalties and interest. I just ignored it for several months because I, emotionally, couldn't deal with it. Finally, I paid it rather than fight it. I ended up hurting my credit score. I wish credit reports took bereavement into account.

I resigned myself to being a listener since I was clueless how to effectively discipline. I tried to be present and be available. I admit to trying to solve problems with money and material things, something that bothered me then and makes me cringe to remember. I tried to stay calm. I talked about Mark with them. I said "I love you" a million times. Still, I felt out of control.

Back at school, on the round table I would set a crate of watercolor sets and large cups holding big paintbrushes. There were a variety of different sized plastic containers and a yellow pitcher holding more water. Several rolls of paper towels stood ready. There was a stack of white drawing paper and oil pastels. I would reach into the white striped cup filled with tongue depressors, each with a student's name on it. I called each student's name as I pulled their stick. That student left the rug where she was waiting, mostly patiently, and took a piece of paper and a set of oil pastels. Students would go to their tables and start drawing. Usually it was a picture that related to something we were studying: whales, the desert, weather. They worked quickly and the room filled with a quiet buzz.

As soon as a child was done drawing, he came to me and said, "I'm ready." I would tell him to take a set of paints and two brushes, one for him and one for his neighbor. I carried water to their table. Only adults could handle water. Breaking this rule meant your paints were taken away.

At this point the room became crazy busy. Ideally, I would have another adult with me but I did it many times by myself. Wet, wet brushes loaded with paint were splashed over the color filled oil pastel drawings. The paper wrinkled where there was no oil pastel. The drawings took on a new dimension. I walked through the room, delivering clean water cups or replacing dirty paint-filled water containers.

"Beautiful, Clementine!"

"Joanie, you better finish your drawing if you want to have time to paint."

"A little more paint, Arthur."

"Oh, Ellie, I think you're done painting. If that paper gets any wetter, it will fall apart."   And so on.

When a painting was finished, it was blotted with paper towel. The desks were dried with another paper towel. "You know what to do," I would say to the artist. She would go to the writing center to get lined paper. Back at her desk, she began writing about her painting.

After the first few writings are stapled to the finished paintings, I hung them on the clothesline across the room or in front of the windows. Then I passed the job to the finished artists. One or two would staple, and another one or two would stand on the wide sturdy stepstool and hang the artwork and writing with clothespins.

A child got the job of collecting paintbrushes. I collected water and poured it into a basin. As students finished, they would go to the classroom library for a book or get their writing folder to write a story. The room was filled with productive voices and happy noise.

Usually, I did this before recess or library or fine arts so I had a minute to finish cleaning up. The work was beautiful, full of bright colorful images. I would grade the writing. If the painting was related to science or social studies, there would be a grade for that, too. There were very few mishaps in this activity because the expectations were made very clear at the beginning. The students knew they would be responsible for their behavior so they rose to the occasion.

I savored the structure I was able to construct in the classroom. It balanced my life. Routine can be a balm when parts of your life have no stability. I recognized the gift it gave to a kid, who like me, had none at home.

I stopped by to visit the third grade one day. "My" kids clamored around, wanting me to acknowledge them. Finally, I asked, "What are you supposed to be doing right now?" They all stood straight, smiled sheepishly at me, and went back to their work. I wandered through the room saying hello, flashing hand signals, and showing one or two the tube of lipstick I had in my pocket.

"This class is so squirrelly," the teacher said to me. "They are only serious during the pledge. Did you teach them that?"

Darn tooting, I did. It was a routine they needed to learn. It's a life skill and they love life skills.

CHAPTER 18

FOLLOWING MY MOTHER'S ADVICE

Amelia and Wendy got in trouble for picking on Jorge in fine arts. They were two well-behaved girls, so getting in trouble was a rarity. Evidently, they kept snarling things like, "Don't touch those scissors. He touched them. Ew!" The teacher took away their recess and said they needed to come to her room to write an apology note. On our way downstairs, Amelia started to cry. Just then, her mom, who was a teacher at the school, came up the stairs toward us. I told her mom what had happened. Her response was, "Ms. Meredith, I promise this will never happen again." Amelia started to sob harder. Her face turned pink and blotchy. She cried so hard she started hiccupping.

When we arrived in the room, I had Wendy give me her agenda to send a note home. I told her it would not be fair to Amelia if her mom knew and not Wendy's. She began to cry also. I gave them both graham crackers mainly because Amelia was crying so hard she had made herself nauseous. The girls gave Jorge his notes after recess. I then instructed them to write "being mean" on a piece of scratch paper. I marched them over to the trashcan where I started tearing up the papers. "We are getting rid of being mean. I never want being mean to be part of your behavior again." I gave them the shredded paper to throw it in the recycling bin. Much to my surprise, they tore the pieces up into tinier pieces before dumping them.

Another bit of mothering advice my mom taught me was: *Pick your battles.* It applies well to life in general. Some things need to just slide off like water on a duck's back, whether at home or at school.

Some years, there were very few battles in the classroom to choose from. Most years there were dozens. If someone is bleeding, fainting or choking, well duh, that's your battle of the moment. Luckily, it's rarely that dramatic.

Jordan was a smart boy. He had several speech issues, but the most obvious was he couldn't say his Rs. This meant he couldn't say his own name correctly. In fact, I never had a single Jordan who could say his Rs. That, compounded with the other issues, made his speech almost indecipherable. He resisted the speech teacher. He didn't like to participate in the speech class because he felt he was smarter than the rest of the kids. He might have been.

The speech pathologist and I decided to call a meeting between Jordan, his mom, and us. Jordan's mom readily agreed. Before the meeting, Jordan told his speech teacher in a very arrogant way, "My mom is going to sign me out of speech."

The speech teacher came to ask me if I thought that was true. I doubted it. Jordan's mom was pretty realistic about her children. I called Jordan over. Here was a bloody battle that I couldn't avoid.

"Jordan, your mom is not going to sign you out of speech."

"Yes, she whiw!"

"No, because she knows you still need help."

"She whiw! It's fo babies!"

"Jordan, you are a really smart boy, but you still can't say 'Jordan' clearly. I think it's important. You can learn to speak clearly, but you have to practice."

"I do so speak kwewy!"

"I'm sorry. I'm not making fun of you, but you just said 'kwewy,' not clearly. Can you hear the difference?" The speech pathologist was standing next to me. I could feel her tension. She didn't want to hurt his feelings. Neither did I, but it was time for a battle, the reality check battle.

"Yes I hiw the diffewence, but no one cahws!" He argued.

"Jordan, honey, I'm so sorry to say this, but you are very hard to understand sometimes." He crawled under my desk and got out the stress box.

The speech pathologist looked sad. "You made him cry."

I hated this. Who wanted to make a nice kid cry? "He had to hear it. He wasn't going to even try unless he heard the truth."

I told Jordan's mom exactly what happened before the meeting. When she came in, Jordan, with hope, said, "Wiw you sign me out of speech? Pweeze."

"Of course not. But if you work hard you might only need to go for a little longer." Looking at us, she said, "What additional work can we do at home? Jordan doesn't need help reading, but we can work on this every day." He didn't like this turn of events, but he accepted he had lost the battle.

Some kids come into the class after a summer of "Whatever!" No one sets expectations. This isn't an income thing. Some of the worst situations were two-parent homes where the little prince or princess ruled the roost.

There was one mom who was consistent. She was consistent about being late. She was consistent about making excuses. In first grade, she brought her daughter, Noelle, Burger

King every day for lunch. I told mom and Noelle: No Burger King

for lunch unless you bring it for all 28 students. That worked. I

also told her what time school started. That didn't work. The

school gave the mom an alarm clock. Twice. The security guard

would go knock on their door a half hour before school started.

Noelle would stroll in 45 minutes late every day. Mom did

manage to drop a Lunchable off to the office in time for lunch

each day. I strongly suggested buying several Lunchables at a

time to save everyone energy. That didn't work either.

Needless to say, Noelle was resentful of the consistency in

the classroom. She mostly went along with the program because

her friends did. She was having trouble academically and never

had her homework done. She was a great artist and I tried to

reward her with time to draw. She was used to being the ruling

princess and cast me in the role of the evil stepmother teacher.

Just shy of a year and a half after Mark's diagnosis, the

celebration of his remission ended. The cancer had metastasized to his liver. Tom was going to Australia on a student trip. Elena

was going to gymnastics camp to start her training as a coach.

Both would be gone two weeks. Tom left on Saturday. Elena left

on Sunday. Mark went to the hospital on Monday morning to

have the half of his liver where the cancer resided removed. It

may have been the longest day of my life.

After several hours of waiting, the surgeon, Dr. Maker,

came out in his surgical green scrubs to speak to me. "I did not

save Mark. I did buy him maybe two years. For now, he'll be fine if

he survives the surgery. There's an 85 percent chance he will."

He left the room. I sat stunned.

My mom and minister Nannene, who had spent the

morning with me, held my hands. Nannene reminded me her

daughter had beat stage four cancer. "They don't know

everything, Lee-Ann."

Mark finally got to the recovery room around 11 p.m. We

were waiting for a room to open in ICU. I sat on a stool next to his

bed in the freezing space and held his hand. I talked quietly to him, reassuring him that he was doing fine. Dr. Maker's comment

kept replaying in my mind. I wanted him to live, so I decided I

wouldn't tell him yet. It would worry him too much. I would save

it until he was a little better.

Mark spent several days in ICU before moving to recovery.

It was two or three days before he could talk. He had drains and

tubes everywhere. Friends would stop by for a moment.   I would

arrive early each morning before rounds. I'd stay through lunch

and be back by dinner. Mark kicked me out around 8 p.m. each

day. He had always needed his alone time and the only time of

day that allowed for it in the hospital was night. That chance to

fall apart when I wasn't there.

Two days before the kids were to get home, Mark was

released. He still had a drain in his side attached to his liver. We

stumbled into the house and he plopped down on the couch. I

fixed some lunch and he moved to our bright sunny kitchen to

eat. "It's such a relief to be home. I can wait a long time before I go back to the hospital." After lunch, I helped him back to the

sofa bed and he slept a while.

When he woke, he was gasping for breath. "I must have

pulled this fucking drain. God, it hurts!" Mark rarely swore. He

was far more inclined to shout "Fornicate, copulate, defecate!"

than drop an F bomb. I put the back of my hand to his neck. He

was burning up.

"Um, you lay here, honey. I need to make a couple phone

calls. I'll be back in a few."

I stepped out of the house and sat on the deck steps. My

hands shook as I called our family practitioner, Doug Stoltzfus. I

explained what was going on. "I'm sorry," he said. "I know this is

hard, but you have to take him back to the hospital. He shouldn't

be running a fever and he shouldn't be in that much pain. Go! I'll

call and let them know you're on the way."

I felt like I wanted to die. I didn't want to go back either.

This was my idea of a nightmare. Mark sobbed as I knelt down to

tie his shoes. I know I said soothing things as we slowly walked out of the house, taking frequent breaks so he could catch his breath. I tried to stay calm as I drove back across the north side of the city.

Mark's lung had collapsed and he had a staph infection. I left to make another round of phone calls to family. When I came back, I had to wrap myself in the special isolation garb. The pulmonary team was about to insert a chest tube. "Do you want me to stay?" I asked Mark.

His eyes rolled at me in misery. "No! Go!" I went into the hall to wait. I could hear his yelps and moans. My heart was breaking. My mind was racing. I was worried sick. The kids would be back tomorrow and I had no idea how to deal with any of this.

Later that day, Mark requested his rubber chicken. It was still in the items in the car from his surgery stay. We hadn't even had time to unpack. We hung it on his IV pole. That afternoon his port for his medications failed. The IV meds had to be put in a pick line on his arm. Those medications included a constant regime of antibiotics and morphine, running up a bill of over

$65,000. He hated taking the morphine and was convinced he'd become addicted to it.

At this point, he was being seen by the surgical team, the pulmonary team, the gastroenterology team, the oncology team, *and* the infectious disease team. Five teams! Doug had arranged for the best doctors in each area to be on Mark's team. When that top pulmonologist came in to see Mark, he asked Mark to cough. Mark coughed. The doctor said, "Again." So Mark said, "Again."

The pulmonologist stood up, stethoscope in hand, and looked at Mark, "Okay, smarty pants. Coughing, not joking."

"But joking never hurts. Coughing does," Mark retorted.

One day, a beautiful, young nurse was fussing around the room. "Will I ever be able to golf after this?" Mark asked.

"Of course."

"Good, I couldn't golf before."

I felt like I was married to Groucho Marx. He always had a joke or a stunt. Afterwards, he had no recollection of these antics.

One morning the pulmonary team ordered an MRI. Mark had prepped by drinking the nasty radioactive stuff needed for the test. Transport came. As Mark was put on the cart, he cussed like a sailor. I stood by, worried. "We hear it all the time, ma'am. It's okay."

"Well, I don't hear it all the time. He is only swearing because of his level of pain." They rolled their eyes at me. I was pissed.

Mark got down to the testing area only to find that the surgical team canceled the MRI. I was done. I was fighting mad and needed to know how to win this battle.

I called Doug Stoltzfus. "What do I do? These teams can't agree on anything. Should I worry? Is he going to die?"

He changed the orders to make sure everything had to go through him first. "Not now. I promise, I will tell you when it's time to worry."

Mark lived through so much pain that month. His sister, Margaret, arrived just as they pulled his chest tube. She sat and held his hand. I went home to spend a few minutes with my kids and hear about their trips. I discovered Tom was not at all interested in talking to me. The fifteen-year-old boy battles had begun and would last six or seven more years.

On August 12, Mark refused another pick line to be started in his arms. On the best of days, it took over a half hour of poking and prodding to find a vein, and he was done. "Give me the meds orally," he told them. If they even tried to start an IV, he threatened to walk out of the hospital.

"Who can blame him?" Dr. Stoltzfus commented.

Mark wanted to be home for his birthday, August 15. The teams were arguing again about when he could be released. Dr. Maker, the surgeon, said yes. The pulmonologist said no. Doug Stoltzfus got the head cardiologist to come in as a tiebreaker. Both doctors agreed they would accept the cardiologist's decision. The verdict was yes! Go home! Heal!

CHAPTER 19

DISCOVER WILDLIFE

"Discover Wildlife: Teach School" is a saying on a cute throw pillow I saw in a catalog. It makes you chuckle. It is true and yet not true. We are all animals, although we try to believe we are a little more domesticated and intellectual than most.

So I think of the zoo. I often felt as if I was a zookeeper or maybe a lion tamer.

Lions. Oh, I've had those. Both male and female. Lazy, smart, nice looking, leaders of the pack. They crook their fingers and everyone is at their beck and call. Usually, they rule the boys in the room. One girl who ruled the boys was the best athlete in the grade and eventually the school. She was a toughie. She battled for the classroom territory with me. I never called on her first because all the boys would follow her lead if she did not like the lesson I was teaching. If this little lioness had suggested the boys jump from our second story window, they would have scrambled for the windowsill, jostling each other in their rush to obey. Lions have power and crave more.

Gorillas. Oh yeah! They beat their chest and growl. They are tough, but they can be surprisingly sensitive. They are moody and often are big crybabies. Gorillas are the most likely to be crybabies in fact.

Penguins. They slip and slide through life. Their attentions spans are brief, but they can be brought back if you have something fun, shiny, or interesting. Oops! There they go. Off the bank again. Splash!

Snakes. Mercifully, there have been relatively few of these, but they surface quickly when I just think "snake." I classify the thieves in this group. One year it was a bit of a snake pit. I had several thieves in the room. They even stole the prizes from the prize box. The smart, cute, all-American snake even sold her stolen prize bouncy balls on the playground after school. Fortunately, most years there is just one snake so it is easy to figure out where things have "wandered" off. Tammy stole my Christmas gifts out of my gift bags. Renée stole things and told her mom I gave them to her. All the classroom scissors? For crying out loud, Mom, get a clue. A box of staples? Really? Her mom made her bring a few staples back just in case I needed them.

Hyenas. They are mean laughers. They get put in a transmogifier, the invention from *Calvin and Hobbes* that turns on being into another, early in the year. They are not the bullies. They are the sidekicks. I put pressure on them to switch into zebras, impalas, or flamingos.

Sloths. I have only had a couple of these. They came into their slothiness due to unbearable babying at home. They licked their desks after lunch, moved at a snail's pace, and grew mold in their fur.

Warthogs. Check.

Anteaters. Check.

Cheetahs. These are the quite children who move so quickly you think you must be seeing things. Oh yeah, they are marvelous!

Monkeys. Check, check, check, check, check. They are the ones who are full of curiosity. They are seekers, trying new things and imitating each other. As crazy as monkeys are, they are charming and smart and just good old-fashioned fun. Or as we said in Room 203:

>Monkey see, Monkey do
>Monkey gets in trouble, too.

CHAPTER 20

SELF-CONTROL! COME HITHER!

Crystal and Juanita were new friends. They had both been the divas of their respective first-grade classrooms. In second grade, they sat at the same table. They chatted and chatted and chatted and chatted. Crystal was much sneakier than Juanita so Juanita was usually the one who got caught talking. I asked her to pick one of my hats to match my outfit and bring it to me.

I put it on. "Juanita, you are a smart girl and I think you like our class. Why won't you stop talking when I ask you to?"

Her eyes got teary. "Crystal keeps talking to me. I don't want to talk."

I beckoned Crystal over. "Crystal, Juanita claims the reason she keeps talking is you are talking to her. Is this true?" Crystal surprisingly admitted that was is true. "What can we do to stop this?"

We agreed that if one of them started talking, the other would put her finger to her lips, signaling her to stop. The girls shook on this.

The next morning, I woke up knowing that the handshake just wasn't going to be enough to stop the constant conversation. When the class came in the room a few hours later, I had the two girls come to me. I told them I didn't think the handshake was serious enough. I wanted a pinkie promise. They both leaned back with shocked looks. They looked at each other and then at me. In case you didn't know, a pinkie promise is pretty serious business. It is binding.

"Well?" I prodded. They both stood up straight and looked each other with serious expressions across their pixie-sized faces and shook on it. It was hard not to burst out laughing so I pushed the glee to a place where I could enjoy it later.

After that, when they started talking all I had to do was show them my pinkie and they stopped.

I wish I had perfect self-control. If I did, I'd be thinner, tidier, and probably so perfect no one would like me. Over these 50-plus years, I spent the first 30 or so beating myself up about my imperfections. Then life taught me an eye-opening lesson.

At 31, I had an almost three-year-old Tom and a six-month-old Elena. It was January 1989. I was working part-time as a bookkeeper for a trust attorney. I got what I thought was my first period after Elena was born. The cramps were unbelievable. I lay on the floor thinking if I stretched out, they would be less painful. I assumed they were bad because of the IUD I had. It got worse. After three or four days, I went to see my doctor. He was older, ready for retirement. I explained about the tremendous pain I was having. I explained about it being the first period since

Elena was born. I told him it was centralized on my right side. He didn't really listen. He told me to schedule a barium enema.

The next Saturday, eight days after the pain started, was the earliest I could get in. The Eastern European tech was disgusted. "Quit being a babee! Vy do you cry? It's not so bad theese test."

The next day, I was in mind-boggling pain. I could no longer sleep in our waterbed. I was determined to go to work the next day because quarterly tax payments were due. I also knew I was dying. I got up during the night to kiss my babies good-bye.

Somehow, I did get up and go to work. About 10 a.m., I started to hemorrhage. My doctor said since I was hemorrhaging I should call the OB/GYN. The OB/GYN said, "Get in here ASAP!"

My boss told a mailroom clerk to take me in a cab to the hospital where the OB/GYN's office was located. The clerk put me in a cab and paid the driver. As he left, he told the driver, "Don't waste any time. She's hemorrhaging," and slammed the door. The cab driver got me there pretty damn quickly.

My wonderful OB/GYN saw me as soon as I got there.
First, he did a pregnancy test. While we waited for the results, he
removed the IUD. I think I fainted at that point. My next memory
was being put on a cart. The doctor stood next to me and said I
was pregnant and he was admitting me to the hospital.

The rest of the next two months is pretty blurred. I had an
ectopic pregnancy that had ruptured. My abdomen was full of
blood and infection. They had removed my badly inflamed
appendix. The late 1980s was a time when everyone was worried
about blood transfusions, so while I qualified, they opted not to
give me one. It meant a much longer recovery time.

Through the blur I realized I still had a purpose for this life.
I could have or should have died. It seemed there were other
plans for me.

Interestingly, my desire for perfection was gone. Maybe it
resided in my appendix and was surgically removed. My healing
was a lightening up process.

As the next several years passed, I worked three days a week and did "mom things" the rest of the time. I was involved in my church and then was a classroom volunteer and PTA member when my kids started at our school. Life was relatively calm and that was fine with me. Who knew I was building reserves for later?

Mark and I always thought we would relocate and live somewhere other than Chicago. I kept using this as my reason for putting off starting work on my teaching certification. One night, my dear, wise friend, Sue Stukey said to me, "You can keep finding reasons not to do it. Wherever you go, they will have teaching programs. Why wait?"

She was right, of course. So I did.

Teaching is a practice. It is an art that requires daily self-control applications. You may be a "natural" teacher, but you still constantly encounter new lessons, behaviors, and conflicts. Hopefully, you learn from each one.

Phillipa was a smart cookie, but she was also a dynamo. Her temper was a thing to behold. One of the boys in the class got under her skin in a way that caused her to turn beet red. One day, he pushed her to the brink and she hurled her box of crayons across the room. Much to her chagrin, this led to a mother/daughter/teacher meeting.

I can still picture her mother sitting looking at Phillipa, one eyebrow raised and a steely look in her eyes. As they left, Phillipa's mom turned to me. "There will be no more of this." Then she winked at me.

There was no more of that. None. Not any. It was over. A month or so later, I told Phillipa I was proud of how she had gotten her temper under control. "How did you do it?" I asked.

"My mom said if she *ever* got another complaint about my temper, she would never make spinach for me again. I love spinach!"

I'm never sure what will help a child find a way to gain the upper hand over a behavior. I had put a handmade sign on the wall that read: *Everyone wants to do their best!*

Bertie had been driving me crazy for several weeks. My patience had run thin. I ranted to Jessica, my student teacher that year. "He is just lazy! He's smart! He's talented but all he does is talk. He's not interested in doing what he is capable of!"

Brave soul, Jessica pointed to the sign. "Everyone wants to do their best. Remember."

"Argh! You're right."

So Bertie and I had yet another conference.

"I'm feeling frustrated, Bertie. You are super smart. You are in a reading and spelling group with your friends. I find books that are interesting for you guys, but you aren't doing your work. Whenever I look at you, even when I'm talking, you're visiting with your friends. You know you are keeping them from listening. What can I do to get you focused?" This was a very long diatribe for a conference. It showed how crazed I was by this situation.

"I don't know." He was sullen.

"Are you bored? I try to find cool stuff for you guys. They're not bored. Am I picking things you don't like?"

"No. The books and stuff are cool."

"What do I need to do?" I put my hands out from the sides of my neck. "Should I give you a cone of shame like in the movie *Up*?"

He looked me in the eye and burst out laughing. I took this as a breakthrough. "Maybe." He chuckled.

I decided to roll with it. "So if I give you this hand sign, will you stop talking and do your work?"

"Sure. I'll try." We shook on it. His behavior completely switched after that. Our common sense of wacky humor turned Bertie into not quite a model student but close.

I used many visual cues as reminders. I looked like a coach on the sidelines using signs to call plays. Some were general signs the whole class knew. Many had come out of a private conference, where the student and I came up with a sign that would help them remember how to behave. There was Bertie and his cone of shame. He laughed every time I did it but settled down. Lowering a flat hand reminded everyone to sit down. A hand on my face would remind Elmer to take his hand out of his mouth, one of his nervous habits. (The other was giggling hysterically. I never did get him to break that habit.) I'd look at Bingo and rub my fingers together to remind him use his scrap of yellow felt rather than put his fingers in his nose. And so on.

Moses liked to pretend to shoot guns all day long. He shot everyone numerous times a day with the sound effects to accompany the action. I tried dozens of things to make him stop. Finally, I drew a gun on a white circle of paper and put a red "No" line through it. He and I taped it on the top of his desk. After that all I had to do was tap the picture and even across the room, he'd stop. I have no idea why it worked but it did.

Each minute and hour of the day, I tried to encourage self-control practice. It took a lot of time. Let's face it. It's as much of a life skill as reading and math.

CHAPTER 21

PARENTS: THE BLESSING AND THE CURSE

In the year when I had my toughest group, the class I lovingly referred to as "Whac-a-Mole," we had a special education annual meeting in October for Lewis. He always had a fancy hairstyle and a toothless grin. During the meeting his mom said, "You know he still drinks a baby bottle at night. His dad gives it to him." I'm certain my jaw dropped to my chest. Everyone else at the table looked equally stunned, but no one else took it up.

"I think I need to meet with Lewis and you next week. What day works for you?"

We agreed to meet right after school a few days later. Lewis was very nervous. When his mom arrived, I said to Lewis, "Do you know why we are meeting?"

"No."

"Lewis, you are eight-and-a-half years old. You have to stop drinking a baby bottle. Tonight. Do you understand?"

His eyes filled with tears. "Yes, and I'll give up my dolls, too."

I groaned inwardly. "No, I'm not worried about your dolls. Maybe they'll make you a wonderful dad someday. The bottle, however, hits the trash. Not the kitchen trash. Your neighbor's dumpster so you can't dig it out later on. Got it?"

He sat crying. "Mom, do you have anything you want to tell him?"

She looked at him with a disgusted look on her face. "You better not say, 'Daddy, if you love me, you'll buy me a new bottle and milk.' You better not!" She sounded like a bossy older sister imitating his whiney voice, not at all like a mom.

I cocked my head at Lewis. "You would say that to your dad?"

"Well, he falls for it." He gave me a smug smile.

He then started crying in earnest so I sent him out for a drink from the water fountain. His mom looked at me. "What do you think is wrong with him?"

I thought, *Lady, you are what's wrong with him.*

A few weeks later Lewis's front teeth started to grow in. He hadn't had front teeth since his first time in kindergarten. "Hey, kiddo. Your teeth are growing in."

"Well, I'm off the bottle now."

Most teachers get frustrated when we hear how we are failing at helping kids. We work so hard. We plan, we teach, we reinforce, we redirect. We give song-and-dance performances to hold attention. We test, teach some more, test again. Surprisingly, no one tells you in teacher training programs that you will be a social worker, too.

What I don't do is: put your children to bed on time. I don't

limit electronics: television, phones, play stations, mp3 players. I

don't read bedtime stories, give baths, talk about the news, give

birthday parties, or take them to the zoo. I don't wake your child

in the morning, check the weather before he gets dressed, fix

breakfast, and get him to school on time.

I have a child about six hours a day. I am not their family. I

am not a student's mommy, grandma, or big sister. I might

become their friend, but I am always their teacher first.

I have been fortunate with the families I have taught. Yes,

I feel like I teach families as well as children. Children in my room

have never been that age before. I know seven-year-olds. So I

teach families about what is typical behavior. Just as with

children, some families are more difficult than others.

Most of my interactions are with the mothers. I know

about being a mother. My son Tom was a gifted student. In all my

years teaching, there were only a handful of kids who were at his

level. Only one or two were higher.

Elena, my daughter, was bubbly, active and sang like a bird on stage in front of the entire school, but she was a struggling student. We discovered in third grade she had double vision and a focusing problem. She went to eye therapy for a few months to correct it, but by then she had lost a lot of ground. She also had ADHD. Since girls manifest that differently from boys, it went undiagnosed until she was in college.

I mothered both sides. Tom was so smart that he was lazy about school. Elena worked her tail off for mediocre grades. I had walked the road of parenthood myself.

Mikael was a sweet little boy. He barely talked. He flinched when I called him to come over to talk to me regardless of the reason. I know that meant he was probably being hit at home. He was in special education and had an aide because he needed constant redirection. He could do most of the work if he could stay on task.

His parents were the lowest functioning parents I ever had. I know mom could read, but she did not begin to comprehend. I would guess that her IQ was about 60 or 65. I am uncertain if dad could read, though. He was dirty and often drunk. He yelled at Mikael all the time. Mikael told his aide stories about his mother being hit by dad including once giving her a black eye. His aide and I watched him all year for signs of abuse, but we never saw any. He never told us of any either. I rarely had a kid I just wanted to take home and raise but he was one.

The spelling homework was a choice each night. One choice was cutting the letters of the spelling words from flyers or magazines and gluing down the word. It was called "Cut It Out!" but I thought of it as "Ransom Words." I explained this homework to Mikael. He and I did it in class. He knew what it was. Whenever he did it at home, however, it was wrong. "Save at Jewel" or "Sirloin Steak" or another random phrase was cut out and glued on his paper. I explained how to do it to the parents. His aide explained it to the parents. His special education teacher explained it to the parents. No luck. I asked him why he didn't tell his mom and dad the right way to do it. He just stared at me and whispered, "I don't know." I took that option off his possible

homework.

Stella was my bully extraordinaire. A couple of girls in the

room wanted so badly to be Stella's best friend. I will never

understand this, but that is how it is. Maybe they thought she was

cool, maybe they thought she wouldn't pick on them, or maybe it

was about being popular.

One of the girls was a beautiful girl with black hair and

blue-grey eyes. Hilary was smart, funny, and flip. She so wanted

to be friends with Stella that she took to doing some bullying

herself. One day, Hilary made fun of the way one of the girls

dressed. I told her I would be speaking to her dad when he picked

her up. I had discussed the bullying behavior with the parents in

the past. Dad was visibly upset when I told him what happened.

The next morning before school, Hilary and her parents

showed up in the classroom. We all sat down to discuss

what could be done. I noticed she was

wearing a standard school uniform, a navy blue jumper with a white polo shirt. Mom said, "I want to apologize for my little darling's behavior. We want you to know this behavior is unacceptable for our family." Dad said, "We reminded her that we have a bigger house that we rent out and live in a small apartment so she and her brother can come to this school because they like it here."

"She has written an apology to her classmate," her mom said. "What do you have to tell Ms. Meredith?"

"I'm sorry," Hilary said, very sweetly. "I won't say mean things to my classmates anymore."

"We explained to her that she isn't just one person," Dad said. "What comes out of her mouth represents her whole family. Neither her mother nor I are mean people. We don't walk that walk. We won't let her behave that way."

"She's a lucky girl who gets to pick what she wants to wear to school," Mom continued.

"Not everyone else has that luxury. So she will be wearing uniform to school until we know she is not being mean. After she proves she can be nice she can wear what she wants on Fridays. How can we check with you each day?"

We agreed on my drawing a smiley face in Hilary's agenda at the end of the day if she had treated her classmates with respect. If she had a week with all smiley faces, she came to school in some cute outfit.

Hilary heard the message loud and clear. She made a remarkable effort to be nice. I was duly impressed by the parents desire to work with me and by setting high expectations for their daughter.

Hooray for responsible parents!

CHAPTER 22

READING (AND EVERYTHING ELSE) IS THINKING

I sat in my rocking chair. A couple dozen seven- and eight-year-olds sat in front of me on the rug. Criss-cross applesauce. Waiting. Their red reading notebooks were in their laps, and pencils were in their hands or behind their ears in imitation of me. I held up a yellow picture book, *Abe Lincoln: A Boy Who Loved Books*.

"Did you know Abraham Lincoln loved books?" Heads shook back and forth. "Who in here loves books?" Every single one of the bright beings raised a hand.

I drew a huge capital T on the chart. Over one half I wrote "Abe." Over the other half, I wrote "Me." I told them to put this in their red reading notebook.

When most of them were finished, I asked, "Reading is?"

"Thinking!" they shouted.

"Great! I want you to think about how you might be like Abraham Lincoln. You might also find ways you are different. You can write them on your chart as you discover them. You already know one way you're alike. Who remembers?"

Some students looked puzzled until they realized they loved books just like Abe did. They write *Love books!* in the notebooks. Stopping frequently, I read the story so they would have time to jot similarities and differences. Everyone was busy. Some peeked at a friend's work to find out how to spell a word. Even the struggling students could find something to write.

When we finished, they studied their T-charts and wrote a paragraph on ways they were similar to Abraham Lincoln, a famous president who was once a child like themselves.

Delilah wrote: *Me and Abe love to read. We both like to wressal. Guess what? He saw a bear and so did I. I am like Abe Lincoln.*

What? I wondered where did Delilah see a bear? Who knows? I was not surprised she liked to wrestle.

There is a subplot of a unit on presidents and leaders. I want them to know that presidents are the leaders of our country and understand how they get elected and who they were. Every year, each class carefully studied the poster of the presidents next to the classroom door. Every chance they got, they were inspecting it. Every year, someone noticed they all came one after the other with no years in between. Every year, someone asked about where Martin Luther King was. Every year, someone noticed all the presidents are men.

Here's the subplot: You can be a child like Abraham Lincoln and you can dream big. You can chart your own course and be something special. You can be something beyond your current reality. Obviously, they will be more than a seven- or eight-year-old second grader, but we can't always see beyond who we are today.

Every year, I told them that when they become president, they need to say, "I owe it all to my second-grade teacher, Ms. Meredith." One of my most touching moments in teaching was when I was attending the bar mitzvah of my former student, The Elf. He asked if I remembered telling him that. I certainly did. "I'm still planning on doing that, you know," he confided.

When Barack Obama, our senator, a fellow Chicagoan, became president, we set up televisions in classrooms to watch the inauguration. Room 203 and a few other classes joined a first grade class in their room. There were 100 or so kids and 10 or 11 adults. We listened carefully to the speech. The kids would turn to look at the teachers, who, to their amazement, were crying. Our children, our students of many colors and races, had no idea what having an African-American president meant to their rainbow of teachers. To us, it truly meant all these little lights in our classrooms could dream big, as big as they wanted.

My own life was in transition at that point in time. I had sold my house, my home of 21 years. It had been a wonderful place for a family and was filled with memories, but it was time to let go. In fact, I had let it go. That was the problem. I had moved a few weeks before the inauguration.

I bought a condo in the center of a busy, fun neighborhood. The economy had tanked. I sold my house for three quarters of the original asking price. I used more savings than I had planned, but I made it. Much to my children's delight, a good friend's daughter and son-in-law bought our home. I moved on December 21, 2008. I filled my new home with only the stuff I wanted, no one else's.

Tom and his girlfriend, Betsy, were expecting a baby boy in early March. Betsy was one of Elena's best friends from Cornell College. Tom was 22 and Betsy was 20. While I felt they were too young, too unprepared, and too new to the relationship, I knew they were both good souls. They both came from loving homes with parents who were or had been committed to each other. At first, I will admit I felt a little like I was in the movie *Knocked Up*.

Tom was, however, finishing his sound recording program. Betsy

had spent the fall in Iowa City to complete the first semester of

her junior year. Betsy was a positive influence. It was, however,

the coming baby that gave Tom a purpose that had been

completely missing from his life.

Tom had spent several years not doing much but partying

and reading. He was supposed to be going to school, but he put

no real effort in it. He felt the classes were pointless. Why go to

school when he could learn all this stuff on his own? He didn't say

it but I knew he believed he was smarter than his teachers. He

probably was. I knew he felt this way because it had taken Mark

until he was almost 40 to get his degree. Mark had also felt he

was smarter than his teachers and the classes were irrelevant. It

made me completely frustrated with Tom since I knew his dad

had regretted not finishing college in his twenties.

What Tom did do was read everything and anything he

could get his hands on. So while much of that time was wasted (make it a pun if you must), he was still thinking. Remember, reading is thinking. He thought and thought in his crazy, brilliant way.

My grandson, Mark, was born on a beautiful early spring day. I was there to see him enter this world. Let me say right now, it is much more fun to be in the audience than doing the work of giving birth. I was still sore the next day. Every time someone said, "Push!" I did. Out of habit, I guess.

That night, a long night for any new parent, Tom said he was surprised and overwhelmed at being the father of a baby boy with his dear dead dad's name. There is something about a baby that makes us let go of our hurt. It loses its sting when your child is there. Being a dad and Betsy's partner brought Tom back to earth.

Mark had written a short note to Tom before he died. It said: *Someday you will realize how much you are loved.* Lisel Meuller wrote a poem about a baby healing a parent's soul. She ends with the line: *Love grows by what it remembers of love.*

Indeed, Tom did begin to realize how much he was loved by becoming a father himself.

That fall, they moved back to Iowa so Betsy could finish school. Some of my friends wondered how I could let them go. The way I saw it, how could I not let them move forward in their lives? They had a plan—it was a loose plan—but the beginning of one. What more could a mother want than a child with a hope for the future? I still want him to keep dreaming big.

Remember dreaming is thinking, also.

CHAPTER 23

WHEN ALL ELSE FAILS, TALK TO THE WALL

There were days when everything turned to chaos. I could have every mechanism in place for things to run smoothly. My biggest troublemaker was out with the flu. I had fun and exciting lessons planned.

My mentor teacher, Ellen Meyers, would state: On Monday, they don't behave because it is Monday. On Tuesday, they don't behave because of the weather. On Wednesday, they don't behave because it's hump day. On Thursday, they don't behave because it's a full moon. On Friday, they don't behave because, obviously, it's Friday.

Ellen was my ideal teacher. She had been Tom and Elena's second-grade teacher. She was creative and willing to learn new things to push her students. I volunteered in her room when my own kids were students. I was wildly, fantastically delighted to be in the room next door to her when I started to teach.

Ellen was wise. She knew seven-year-olds. She understood what worked for second graders and what didn't. "They just won't rewrite a story. If you tell them to, they will either cry or start a completely new story. You can trick them by giving them fancy paper, though."

We shared ideas. She was an expert on working with small groups and centers. She was the person who taught me to hide all my crap in a bin before open house or a conference. After school, we would sit and talk about the kids. We discussed what was working, what wasn't, and how to fix it.

Ellen retired at the end of my second year. Mark was still alive. In fact, most of that year, he seemed to be doing better. Ellen was physically exhausted, though. She said she knew it was time to quit the day she had stopped at Jewel on the way to work.

It was almost Passover and she wanted to get her shopping done

while she still had energy. Teachers always have bags and bags of

stuff to bring in each day. She lugged all her school bags up to the

second floor and into her classroom that morning. When she sat

down breathlessly and started to unpack them, she discovered

she had carried up a grocery bag with ten pounds of potatoes in it

for her Seder at home.

As a teacher, the thing I liked to do best was, well, teach. I

was a natural. As a six-year-old, I came home from first grade and

taught my four-year-old sister Linda what I learned. Then I had

her do my homework. So on days when my students forced me to

become simply crowd control, it made me grumpy.

I could resort to yelling. I have many times. Nearly always,

it was because I was frustrated and I had lost my center. As soon

as I did it, I found myself taking a breath to calm myself down and

tried to figure out how to bring myself and the class back into appropriate behavior. I would look up my sleeve to see what tricks I have stored there, grab one, and proceed.

It might have been a change of scenery moving from our desks to the rug or vice versa. It might be a quick sight word spelling test. It might have been putting their heads down on their desks to calm down and refocus. (No, I didn't put mine down; I just breathed deeply and tried to find the ability to smile.) Sometimes I had them draw a picture or do a mundane workbook page to bring the energy back to where it should be. Ellen taught me that trick. "Sometimes they just need to do something mindless to settle down."

When Ellen left, I found the other second-grade teachers were far more "traditional" than she and I were. I was very worried about being the only artsy-fartsy hands-on teacher in my grade. I wanted to stay the course and keep trying to be a best practices teacher, a teacher who wanted learning to be authentic and not scripted. I asked her how I could do this.

"You are going to have to be the humanist. Each of these children is a person who needs help at his own level. Stick to your guns!"

Whenever I felt as if I was fighting a hopeless battle, I remembered that charge. I'd take a deep breath and use that inhalation to give me the nerve to speak my mind. There were days it was mighty frustrating. I often felt I was talking to a wall.

I kept doing my "humanist" teaching. Ellen wasn't referring to the word in a religious sense. Instead, she meant that each child was a human, not a number or a little robot. This is a hard way to teach. Expecting everyone to be able to do the same thing is much easier.

The best compliment I ever got as a teacher was a day when the principal was reading me the riot act over something I had said in a meeting. I felt she had misconstrued what I had meant. Her exact words were, "You are the new Ellen Meyers. Everyone listens to what you have to say. You have to think before you talk." I was still mad, but the Ellen Meyers balm was, oh, so soothing.

Ellen was great at keeping a class busy with a wide variety of work. Things can quickly get a little crazy. This is a three-ring circus act and it's not easy to do. While humor works most of the time as a management tool, sometimes something different is called for. Sometimes the angels would whisper in my ear and an answer to class control became so apparent it startled me.

One year, I had a little boy who had moved to Chicago from Texas. It was an afternoon in early December and it had started to snow. Not a few little skimpy flakes. Big, fat, wet flakes tumbled down. The class went nuts. They always do when it is the first snow of the season. "Santa's coming!" "Christmas!" "Snow! Snow! Snow!"

"Yep! It's December. You've all seen snow before. Sit down. We have math to do." Then I noticed Terry bouncing up and down on his toes. His eyes were as wide as saucers. I realized that no, we all hadn't seen snow, had we?

I sent Cara, the aide in my room that year, down to check how wet it was on the track (a painted oval on the blacktop playground). "We can run on it," she whispered to me.

"Okay, boys and girls. Here's the deal: Terry has never seen snow. So if we go outside to run a few laps, do you promise to come back and work super hard at your math?" Of course they promised. Who wouldn't?

We bundled up. I called the office to tell them we were running outside. "In the snow?" they asked. Terry's classmates were explaining how to catch snowflakes on your tongue as we walked through the building to the playground door.

Their excited faces glowed as they ran through the flakes. The smiles were wide, eyes bright. They chattered and laughed. Terry gazed at the flakes as he ran. Everyone's tongues darted in and out of their mouths in search of snowflake snacks.

They were as good as their word when they came back. They were chill, I guess you could claim. We got done with two math lessons instead of one.

The year after Ellen left, Mark was in hospice at the end of the first semester. I was overwhelmed with the huge pile of paperwork to do. I was sorely missing Ellen's camaraderie. Her advice on handling that crazy wild group would have been wonderful.

One morning, I stood at my desk helping a student and felt like crying about the amount of things to do: grades, reading groups, lesson plans, go to the hospital after work, get Elena here and Tom there. Suddenly, Ellen was standing next to me. "Go do paperwork. I'll cover your class." She had come to school to do just that. There was no one on earth I trusted more to get what needed to be done right. She went and sat in the rocking chair and finished the lesson I was teaching. I think the wall had been listening and had sent her a message.

Some days, after every other trick has been shaken out of my sleeve, I pulled out the last card. I sat very still for a second. The class would slowly realize I'm quiet. I looked up at the wall and called, "Wall? Are you listening? I hope so. No one else is."

The foreheads furrowed. The voices stopped. They looked at me like little cocker spaniels with their heads tilted and questions in their eyes. One or two chuckled. A wiggler shouted incredulously, "I was listening!"

We would move on. Focus was back. This card can't be played very often. But *shabam*! It worked every time.

CHAPTER 24

THE WALL

I stood next to a hospital bed set up in my living room. My 47-year-old husband lay in it, drifting in and out of a morphine-induced sleep. His breath was ragged and his open eyes rolled. Our big yellow cat, Pie, curled between Mark's once skinny legs that had grown to be the size of tree trunks. Pie had chosen to be Mark's partner through this part of his journey.

I was at home instead of in my classroom. The day before I had told my principal this was it. It was only a matter of days now. Hours maybe. She had walked away crying. I had climbed into my car, tough and determined to drive the half-mile home without tears.

Holding his hand, I said, "It's okay, Mark, you can go. We'll be okay. I'll take care of the kids. I'll be fine. We'll meet again just like we did in this life. You know it's true."

We struggled through the day. The substitute hospice nurse was coming in the morning to refill his morphine pump. The clear plastic refill bag plump with liquid relief lay in the refrigerator waiting.

I recall nothing else of that day until about midnight. I called the hospice and explained Mark was groaning in pain. The night nurse talked me through the steps to increase the morphine flow on his pump. He quieted down a little.

An hour later, I checked his pump only to discover he was quickly running out of morphine. I worriedly appealed to hospice again. The woman on the phone said they would send someone to our house. I waited, not very calmly. I kept checking the gauge until around 4 a.m. when the morphine ran out completely and Mark began to moan in earnest. Still no nurse.

It was his Y2K bug. That's what he named it, his cancer. As a techie, he had to be up and on the computer at midnight when the year 2000 came. If there were problems, he would be scrambling to solve them. He was sick. I have thrown away the pictures from that New Year's Eve. I could no longer bear to see how sad, worried, and uncomfortable he looked.

January 13, 2000, he convinced the doctor to tell him the test results on the phone. It was a Thursday evening and Mark was driving home from work, stuck in traffic as usual. When he got home, he sat in his favorite chair and sobbed and sobbed. I felt somewhat impatient with him as I tried to calm him down. Cancer didn't mean death. We could fight it, I claimed encouragingly. Life can change in an inkling, end in a snap. He had to realize he could win. It was the beginning of my three years as a cheerleader. I had to convince him and everyone else this was a war we'd win.

He had walked into class ridiculously late. I was across the room and like everyone else, looked up to find out who had walked in the door. Tall, dark curly hair, a disheveled trench coat with loaded pockets, and a Dr. Who scarf *a la* Tom Baker made the picture as he looked left and right to figure out where he could sit. He held a porkpie hat in his hand and had a leather satchel over his shoulder. What caught me by surprise were the bright blue twinkling eyes. Incredible! My soul must have recognized him and I was smitten.

At break from a class, I stood talking to Scott, my friend from several classes. The ridiculously late man joined our conversation. He worked with Scott at First Chicago Bank.

We talked nonstop. After class we rode the El home to the Fullerton stop. As I got on the bus to finish my trip home, he asked if I'd like to go out. Sure. Of course! Yes, I answered. On the bus, I realized I didn't even know his name.

He didn't show up to class the next week. At break, Scott told me Mark had called him and asked him to let me know he had the crud and would be there next week. Scott beamed at me.

"What's the crud?" I asked, already filled with a sinking feeling

because I had dated another Mark for three and a half years and

that hadn't turned out well.

"Beats me. It sounds as if he likes you. Do you want to go

out with someone with crud?"

"I'm not sure."

That was February of 1980. We did go out the next week.

He didn't know my name either.

Even when you know your husband is going to die, the

finality of it is hard to conceive. I could not bear to watch the

funeral home people carry Mark out of the house. I went and hid

in my bedroom, only mine now, not ours anymore.

I wanted to take a nap since I had been up all night. I

couldn't sleep. A queue of teenagers wandered in the house and

up the stairs to the bedrooms. First Natalie. Her dad went and got

Nat out of school to be with Elena. Russell showed up next. When he got Tom's call on his cell phone, he walked out of school and

took the train to our house. All day more people came in and out.

I was clueless who the myriad of people coming and going from

my home were. I couldn't have cared less.

The next morning, someone came and took the hospital

bed from the living room and the kids and I moved our furniture

back to their old familiar places.

The church was filled to the brim for the memorial service.

People were standing in the back. My brother, Adam, talked

about knowing Mark longer than he had known our dad and

loving him just as much. This took my breath away. Don talked

about Mark not just as his brother but his friend, too. Mark's co-

worker Patty said he had claimed if he lived, he would follow a

call to chaplaincy. She thought he had been her chaplain already.

Art recalled seeing Mark across the El tracks at the Lake Street

stop. He said, "Mark's eyes lit up with the recognition of the joy of

connecting with another life." Art laughed about going outside on a bitterly cold, subzero day with Mark to see if water would

vaporize before it hit the ground. It did.

Someone from church told the story of Mark making an

announcement one Sunday for a work party. First, someone

came up with a lamp. Next, a different person screwed in the light

bulb. Someone else put on the lampshade. Another person

plugged in the lamp. Finally, yet another person turned on the

light. Mark leaned into the microphone and said, "Many hands

make light work."

Marcy, my professional clarinetist sister-in-law, played

When the Saints Go Marching In. In the middle of the song, her

clarinet squeaked. She stopped, eyes brimming. "That was

Mark!"

Mark's death left a hole in me. Some days it was a tiny

thing or more like tiny things: a sieve with the juice of my life

dripping through. Other times, those little holes all joined

together to become big enough to drive a Mack truck into it.

Those were the "sit in the corner and cry" days. The sieve days were more the like little Dutch boy trying to hold the dam together until help came.

These are the things I miss about Mark:

Kisses, small or passionate, both equally.

His hands. They were lovely once he quit biting his nails. I picture them typing on a computer, chopping vegetables, talking, sawing, raking, writing notes, pretending to be covering his mouth and nose for a sneeze only to launch a piece of hidden lettuce across the table with an "Achoo!" I miss holding those hands.

His jokes and his remarkably quick wit. He was the most annoying pun maker. He'd start and go on for hours. You'd thankfully think he had stopped only to have him pop back in the room or call you on the phone with another groaner. There was a hiking trip with the kids a year or two before he died where he went on with bird puns for hours. The more we begged him to stop, the more he came up with followed by a silly chuckle. He

cracked himself up. No, I should say, he *crowed* about it.

He had an incredible way of using humor to check

people's bad behavior. One winter day when the area around the

living room trashcan was littered with dirty tissues, Mark called a

family meeting. *Clunk!* He put the blue flowered trashcan on the

coffee table. Holding a box of Puffs, he started wadding them up

and throwing them at the can. "I guess I was confused," he said,

enunciating each word carefully. "I thought the idea was to get

the tissues in the garbage. Who knew I was so wrong?" We

laughed until we cried. No more dirty tissues were found on the

floor after that meeting.

I miss his love for his kids, any kids, and his desire to be

one with them. He was a kid magnet. They adored his sense of

play. I instantly think of his dressing up for Halloween with a crazy

mask that had a cigar attached or flying the emergency back-up

kite that lived in the trunk of the car. We always had a stash of

bubbles to blow. He would sometimes simply hide behind a tree, frequently little skinny trees, to jump out at us. We laughed

because it was so ridiculous. He would pretend to walk into a

pole, smacking the pole to make a clang! Then he would cover his

nose and groan, "Ow!"

He believed you could never go wrong with good

manners. Never. He baked cookies as a thank you or a bribe for

his co-workers. He was self-effacing yet gracious, charming and

always kind. (Although I'm sure his younger sister, Margaret,

would not agree.)

Most of all, I miss that twinkle in his eyes, that look he

gave when something or someone piqued his interest. It was

there the first time I saw him as he arrived late to our Money and

Banking class. I fell in love with that man with just that look.

There is a picture his sister took at a party in a room at The

Canyon Inn. There are several people in the picture doing a

variety of things. Mark is sitting on the edge of a bed, looking at

someone across the room, twinkling. In fact, I know why he was

twinkling.

He took his search for adventure to a new realm when he died. I can't see the path he walked into the beyond. I'm sure he left a trail marked for me to follow when I go. I can wait a long time to take that road.

We had this crazy common dream. Not a wish but a nighttime dream. The weird thing was we saw it from a different vantage point. It was a garden full of ancient marble art. The garden was beautiful with weeping trees, ferns, and flowers around a reflecting pond. I saw myself on the garden path looking up at a boy who was sitting on the wall. This boy was wearing a simple white tunic-type outfit. I've had this dream for as long as I can recall—since I was a little girl.

Mark, also, had this dream of the same garden since childhood. Trees, pond, path, flowers are all there. The marble artwork was there, too. In his dream, Mark was sitting on the wall watching a girl walk the path.

When Mark died, I told him to go to his beautiful place. I believe it is a Native American tradition to tell a dying thing to do just that. I knew where I was telling Mark to go. That's where I imagine that he waits for me, a boy sitting patiently on a garden wall. Watching.

I moved on to fill in many of the holes with pieces of Mark. His jokes became my jokes. His sense of play became a huge part of me. The knowledge of his love for me and our kids kept me moving forward. I carried those repair patches with me and secured them to my being with the super glue called second grade.

CHAPTER 25

LUCKY GREEN BALLOON OF CHANGE

Slanted green eyes, somewhat pointy ears, and a decidedly impish behavior defined Jan. He argued with me in a disconcerting, unfocused way that made my head spin.

He once tried to start an argument with a student teacher by saying, "Hew don't like me because I'm Czech." He always spoke with a heavy Eastern European accent in a remarkably demanding voice.

"No, I'm from that part of the world, too, Jan," the student teacher calmly replied.

"Hew don't like me because I can't read any gut," he countered.

"You'll learn to read. You'll see."

"Then hew don't like me because I have beeg eears."

She stared at him, astonished. I stepped in at this point. "Get in line, Jan. We are going to gym."

Frankly, more than once I considered stapling those "beeg" ears to the wall.

When he was in trouble, which was nearly every day, I would stop and try to reason with him. "Look at me, Jan. I know you can get this done..." Within a couple of seconds, he no longer looked at me but instead he was ogling my jewelry.

"Nyssss pin, Ms Meredith," or "Ware did hew get tose earrinks? Tae are pretty." Aaargh! He was either going to be a jeweler or a burglar. I was hoping for the jeweler.

One morning, I came back after a day off. Dr. Nelson, the principal at that time, stopped by the room before school. A child in the news had recently choked to death on a balloon and we were discouraging the use of them at school.

She leaned toward me. "I saw Jan on the playground an hour before school started yesterday. He was on the top of the slide with a huge florescent green balloon. He hadn't tied it. He was just holding it shut. I asked him to empty it and give it to me."

"But Mrs. Dr. Nelson! Eet iz my lucky green bahloon," he had told her.

"Let the air out and give it to me now!"

So, he did. Much to her shock and dismay, it wasn't a balloon at all. It was a florescent green condom.

"Lee-Ann! Yuck! Where did he get that thing? Florescent green! Can you find out how he got it? He told me his mother bought it for him." We both laughed shakily.

I hustled Jan from the group as soon as he arrived. "What is it with you and balloons? You know you aren't allowed to have them at school. Dr. Nelson told me what happened yesterday."

"Eet was my lucky green bahloon," he said, pouting.

"No balloons at school! You know that. And where did you get it? Don't tell me your mother gave it to you. I know when you aren't telling the truth."

"Awl right! I found eet behind the seeet of my fahter's truck. He doeseent know I tuke eet. He might be mad I stole heez bahloon."

Ew!

I prayed to find a way to be patient with Jan. He made me absolutely crazy. He also made me laugh. He was just so wildly bizarre. I'm not sure if I was usually shaking my head in disbelief or twitching. When I think about him, I just laugh. At the time he was a tough kid to handle. In retrospect, he was a present tied up with a bow. I learned many things from him, not the least of which was patience.

I had many tough students, many wigglers, many worries. Multiply that three or four times, and you'll see how many wonderful, lovely, funny children come from rock solid homes. Most of the children I taught were getting free or reduced lunch because of their economic status. They were rich, however, in the love they received. Many of my students had cousins or even aunts or uncles in another classroom.

Once, on a day after a field trip, a mom came to tell me she was worried about Arthur. During the field trip, he had told her he hated his uncle because his uncle always beat him up. The mom had told the principal and she thought we should call the Department of Children and Family Services. The mom looked shocked when I laughed. "His uncle is only nine years old. He's Arthur's best friend," I explained.

A few years ago, if you'd ask me who I was, I would have said a second-grade teacher and a mom. The teacher part would have been first. The mom was second but still important. I was a mom of more than my two children. I was a second mom for many of their friends. In fact, I was more reliable than some of their actual moms. My home was full of young adults laughing, talking, and sleeping. Both roles, mom and teacher, kept me young.

The teacher part was always about the passion to teach. The children filled most of my waking moments. They were in my dreams at night. I tried to think of ways to reach them and challenge them.

After the move to my condo, my life began to shift. I took ballroom and swing dance lessons at the Old Town School of Folk Music, three blocks from my new home. Dancing filled me with joy. I always left the class with a smile on my face that lasted at least a day.

I became a Reiki practitioner, eventually becoming a master. I had always been psychic, aware of things unseen. What my mom referred to as a gut feeling was exceptionally strong. I had known this about myself for a long time. When Elena was born and the nurse gave her to me for the first time, the thought that popped in my head was, "So little one, we meet again." I knew who and what I was but had avoided dealing with it. Now was the time to start listening to the guides the Universe had given me.

I felt more adventurous. I traveled a little on my own. I know many women who have done this, but in my mind I was still little Lee-Ann Schutz from Crown Point, Indiana.

On the eighth anniversary of Mark's death, I was driving to Michigan. For weeks, every time I opened a magazine or turned on the TV, there was something about Turkey or Istanbul. As I drove down the highway, I sent the thought whizzing out to the Universe, "If I'm supposed to go to Turkey send me a sign."

I turned on the country road to my cottage. Something large moved on the side of the road. I braked then stopped the car as nine wild turkeys crossed the road in front of me. There were so many of them, I counted. It wasn't until later when I turned on the computer and there was a picture of the Hagia Sofia, I wondered if I would get a sign. Talk about a head-smacking moment.

I planned my trip. I was a nervous but off I went. Each day, I joined a different tour group and met people from around the world. What we had in common was English. I visited Ephasus and Cappadocia, both places that felt wildly familiar to me. I am

sure if I have had prior lives, many of them have been in Turkey.

On my last morning in Cappadocia, I sat and ate my huge Turkish

breakfast under ancient Troglodyte dwellings. Dozens of hot air

balloons filled the bright summer sky. It was an astonishing

moment that filled me with unmitigated joy.

Realizing I could be whoever I wanted to be shocked me. I

wasn't sure what that was yet. Wasn't I a second-grade teacher

extraordinaire? I did not need to meet anyone's expectations but

my own.

Each child gave me joy. Even the well-behaved darlings

had tough days. My rock solid Joanie could be counted on for

anything. I teased her about all the trouble she caused. In reality,

she never caused any trouble. At least not until the day a first

grader barfed on Joanie's feet on the way into the auditorium for

an assembly. Joanie lost it. She threw back her head, screaming,

with tears pouring down her face. The whole school turned to

stare. The barf splattered all over her new super cute shoes.

Fortunately, it was winter and she had boots upstairs in the classroom. We got clean socks from the office and someone retrieved her boots. She moved on.

One classroom trick I had was quiet spray. It was simply a squirt bottle of lavender scented water. When the class was noisy, I sprayed them. They always quieted down after the initial flurry of silliness. I was known to spray down Calvin's, Eleanor's, Nelson's or any other wiggler's desks.

Esparanza was a tough little cookie. She was a tomboy who despised girlie things. She was very funny and caustic but her fuse was short. When she became frustrated, she howled and howled and howled. It was ear splitting and exhausting for everyone. One day in frustration, I sprayed the quiet spray over her head and it misted over her. She took another breath to howl and all the tension went out of her. Could it have been the spray? After a few more howl stopping squirts, I knew it was. Esparanza became a proverbial poster child for aromatherapy.

One morning she stomped into the classroom twenty minutes late. "I haven't had breakfast," she growled.

"Would you like a graham cracker? Or you could go downstairs and get something to eat."

"No! But I think you better give me a squirt of the quiet spray!"

Clementine was one of the gems of my very difficult class. Her goal in life was to be a cheerleader. She had the right positive, perky attitude to be the best kind of cheerleader. She was hardworking, a good friend to her classmates and a joy to have as a student. I would sing the song "Clementine" to her. She'd roll her eyes and laugh with delight. Her best friend, Martha, was just as bubbly and wonderful.

Clementine was one of the many R-less students I taught. Thanks to Barbara Walters, CPS had determined that speech services were not necessary for just not saying the R sound. Clementine didn't qualify for assistance. (I expect she will handle her lack of R with as much aplomb as she does most things.)

A week before school was out for summer, Clementine came to me with a worried expression. Martha was close behind, rubbing her hands in concern. Clementine crooked her head at me. "Ms.Mewedif, can I ask you a question?"

"Sure, Clementine. What's up?"

"Who is the weally, weally, weally, weally, weally nicest teacha at Moofy School?"

With an aghast look on my face, I replied, "Clementine! I am!"

She put her hands on her hips and coolly regarded me for half a minute. Martha's hands dropped to her side and she began to shake her head. Clementine's mouth started twitching. She began to giggle.

"No, Ms. Mewedif. Yo da funny one."

It was one of the best compliments I had ever received. I began to laugh with the girls. It worked for me. Whoever that was.

CHAPTER 26

LIPSTICK KISSES AT THE HARBOR

"Blood? Phooey! Where do you get such ideas?"

At the last Community Sing of the 2011-2012 school year,

I was reading my favorite book, *Wempires* by Daniel Pinkwater, to

the school. I had loved this silly book since I had gotten if for Tom

when he was a kindergartener. The main character wants to be a

vampire but his parents discourage him. One night, vampires

show up in his bedroom saying, "How's 'bout you, Sonnyboy?"

With their heavy accents, they call themselves Wempires. They

wear Converse high tops and drink ginger ale instead of blood.

"Phooey! From television you get such ideas!" they exclaim. They

go to the kitchen and eat and drink. They burp loudly and make a huge mess. The mother shows up and throws the vampires out.

She says, "Now you see why your father and I don't want you

acting like a vampire."

I've read it dozens of times each year with crazy voices. It

was a beloved story of any child who has ever been in Room 203.

I carried the book to the auditorium before school. I was a

bundle of nerves. I knew "they" had something planned for me.

As I locked the door to Room 203, I stopped. I didn't want to cry in

front of the whole school. I unlocked the door and re-entered the

stifling 82-degree room. I stuffed my pockets with tissues. My

theory was if I had them, I wouldn't need them.

The fine arts teacher asked the 600-plus kids in the

auditorium to stand if Ms. Meredith had ever been their teacher.

Almost a quarter of the students and some adults who had spent

time in my room stood and waved at me.

Before school had started, I had stopped in the

auditorium. The words to a song they had written were on the

screen on stage. It was to the tune of "This Little Light of Mine."

That had been a relief to see that. I had been concerned I would

choke up. I knew I would be okay since I despise that song.

Perhaps I should say I despise the namby-pamby way it is sung.

Here is this wonderful protest song that was meant to tell the

world you can't make me hide my light away. Instead it is sung to

make preschoolers feel happy. It is a song to empower not to

pacify. I cringed every single time I heard it.

　　Surprisingly, my usual shoot-my-mouth-off self had never

told the fine arts teacher. I knew her feelings would be hurt if I

did. She had worked hard with all my past and present students

to write it. The "We'll Miss You, Ms. Meredith" version mentioned

the stories I told, the lipstick kisses for which I always expected to

get in trouble, and all the laughter we shared. I'm glad I didn't tell

her because now I could stand there and listen to a love song

written to me without bawling like a baby.

　　I didn't cry but I passed all the tissues out to the people

who did. Afterwards, two seventh-grade boys came up and

hugged me. "You can kiss our cheeks, Ms. Meredith. We promise not to wipe the lipstick off." The tears started to fall while I laughingly kissed their cheeks. I had to beg a tissue from somebody else.

After 13 years in Room 203, I made the decision to walk away from teaching. At least for a year. It was a choice that snuck up on me. I had the feeling for a couple years that I needed some type of change. I hadn't considered just taking time off. Maybe a different room or a different grade was all I had really considered.

In March 2012, the second-grade teachers were hosting a teacher breakfast in Room 205. I was sitting at a table with Maria and Sonia. Sonia had taught second grade for a couple of years and we had been quite the team. Maria started as an aide in Elena's kindergarten class. She started as a classroom teacher the same year I did. They are best friends and were both teaching third grade that year.

Maria leaned forward. "When are you taking a leave of absence, Lee-Ann?"

I was startled to hear myself say, "Next year, I think." At that very moment I decided to hit the 401K to make it happen.

Maria moved to the chair next to me. This was a conversation to whisper, not to broadcast across a room.

"I think it's time. Mark was diagnosed with cancer my first year teaching. My kids are grown. My mom is moving into a nursing home. My classroom was a great place to hide, but it's time to leave the hidey-hole." A weight that I didn't even realize I had lifted off me.

I went to the library to tell Michelle. She is my good friend, a former second-grade cohort, and someone I trusted implicitly. "I'm a little surprised at myself," I told her.

Looking a little surprised herself, she said, "Good for you!"

I sat in Chris Zelenka's office. I broke the news to her and gave her my reasons. It was time to venture out of my room. Her eyes teared up. "Are you sure? Will you be back?"

"Yes" and "I'm not sure" were the answers.

I stopped in Alisa Lee's room. Penny was there. I had been

stoic all day, managing to avoid crying. These two women were

my dear friends of many years. But it was especially hard to tell

Penny. Penny had been diagnosed with colon cancer six months

before Mark. A few days after Mark's diagnosis, Penny and her

husband, Tim, invited us over for dessert. Once Mark had finished

wrestling with the younger kids, we sat at the dining room table

and talked. Penny told Mark he'd now know what morning

sickness felt like. She explained that was a side effect of the

chemotherapy usually used for colon cancer. Losing your hair

wasn't. Tim told me not to be surprised if I became depressed. It

was very hard facing the spouse's illness and a situation you have

very little control over.

Over time, Penny and Mark would compare ports and PET

scans. We rejoiced over Penny's clear status. She brought dinner

when Mark's status wasn't so clear.

A few months after Mark's death, I ran into Tim as I went

into the school auditorium. His face showed a myriad of

reactions: relief Penny was alive, sorrow Mark wasn't, guilt for feeling relief and genuine concern for me. It was a wildly poignant moment that was imprinted on my memory. I wished I was standing in his shoes rather than my own. I had no resentment, only a longing for Mark to have shared Penny's outcome.

I realized while I talked to Penny, it was time to leave my safe haven. I had built a harbor to rebuild myself in Room 203 after Mark's death. School had provided that wonderfully safe place for me.

Within a week, I informed most of the staff, one person at a time. The rumors were flying. Most people thought I was going because I was burnt out. I wasn't, but I *was* sick of the way the media talks about teachers. That wasn't why I was leaving. I was sick of the huge, tremendously time-consuming fights I had to stage to get any child additional help if they were a struggling student. That wasn't it either.

Frank DeJohns first asked if I was emotionally okay. He was worried about me. I told him I was fine. He and I had been through many journeys beginning on that fateful September 11,

2001. Since he taught third grade most years, we had shared

many students. He cried. I hadn't expected that. When I left the

room, I turned and said, "You know I love you, right?"

"Yep. I love you too."

I said "I love you" many times over the next few months. I

reassured many people the school would be fine without me. I

hugged and hugged until my shoulders ached. Chris jokingly

refused to sign my resignation paperwork.

I started teaching as a happily married woman who had

attained her dreams. Now I was a single, middle-aged woman

with grown children who were relatively settled in their lives. Tom

and Betsy were getting married that summer. My grandson, the

new Mark Meredith, was three. Elena was moving away to an

island in Lake Michigan with her boyfriend. He had been Tom's

good friend since middle school and there was a sense of the

permanence about that relationship. Elena's best friend, Jessica,

who had lived with us for a year was moving into her own place.

My mom was ill and we weren't sure how much longer she would be around. It was time for me to figure out my dreams and follow them.

My student teacher, Jessica Petertil, reminded me of the quote by William G.T. Shedd, "A ship is safe in a harbor, but that is not what ships are for." It was time to sail away.

The only time I choked up at school was when I talked to the people who remembered Mark. It took me a while to realize the sea beyond the harbor would allow me to fully grieve my lost life. Then it would bathe me in the cool, soothing recognition of what I had become.

Leaving was so weird. I felt like a teenager leaving for college. I'd been there in some ways over 20 years. Mr. Z. claimed, "We may not have the highest test scores but we have the nicest kids." He believed it and he was right. It was proved to me many, many times.

At some point in those early parent years, I remembered I had always wanted to teach. Second grade, in fact. Suddenly, the flame to teach was lit. How had it all worked out? How had I

ended up with wonderful Ellen Meyers as a mentor? I joked about

doing fertility dances in the hall to get a classroom at that school.

I think the stars aligned and there I was in Room 203 teaching

second grade. My destiny? I think so.

Now, after so many years, it felt so right to leave. I was

stunned, however, by how the community reacted. I knew I was a

straight shooter and was forever trying to be honest in my

communications with everyone I worked alongside: students,

parents, teachers, and principals. I hadn't realized how much of

an impact I had made on them. I had somewhat anticipated the

kids' and parents' behavior. My co-workers' behavior floored me.

It was as if I was lifted up on their shoulders and given a huge

"Hurrah!" I was surprised and humbled by the outpouring of love I

received.

It became apparent I would be quitting, not taking a leave

of absence, because the Chicago Board of Education policies

made it nearly impossible to take leave. I was sad and frightened to make that decision. I was truly excited about the future. The fear of failure, however, was terrifying. My mental image was jumping off a cliff. Could I trust enough to jump without a "leave of absence" bungee cord?

I heard the Universe say to me, "Your angels will catch you." I took one long, last look at where I had been, then I stepped into the unknown with my wide open so I wouldn't miss a single thing.

CHAPTER 27

BUDDHA

Buddha: A teacher is just a boat to take the student over

the river.

Each school year is an adventure. As Buddha teaches, it is

a boat ride across the river of second grade. Some crossings are

smooth with relatively few rough waters. Others are running

rapids nearly every day.

Rivers were a concept my Chicago kids couldn't quite

grasp. Even the idea of "lake" was distorted. The rivers in Chicago

are mostly hidden, seen from a bridge or at a park, guarded by a

chain link fence. They tend to be dirty and slightly "frowned" upon. Poor Chicago River, no wonder it is one of the most polluted rivers in the United States.

Our lake, Lake Michigan, is like an ocean without the salt or tides. Not a lake teaming with life, although some of my families did fish in it. It was more accessible but still a distorted view of a typical lake.

Our water was mostly from the tap or puddles or flooded streets or most likely flooded basements. We are far removed from the world of Buddha and his river.

An overland journey feels more realistic. Up a mountain or hill. Oops! These don't really exist in Chicago either. We are truly flatlanders. My son crashed his bike the first time he rode down a hill on a camping trip. His dad and I watched him take his feet off the pedals and we ran to pick up the pieces of the inevitable oncoming crash. His nose pouring with blood, with skinned knees and legs he sobbed, "I didn't know how to stop."

Rivers, lakes, oceans, hills, and mountains are worthless analogies to a Chicago school child. It is a journey of desks, chairs, rug sitting, spilled lunches, fights with friends, new stories, new skills, and lots and lots of new words, as many as you can ponder. The "horizon," a word taught in second grade, is always in the distance, but it is obscured by the report card pick up, double-digit subtraction, the death of a grandparent or the family dog. (Equally important to someone who has lived their entire life with either Rover's or Abuelo's unconditional love.) We build rivers of thought. They float through the concepts of community, immigration, holidays, presidents, and heroes.

We swim in the calm or rough lakes of stories that help us understand how we belong to each other and the world around us.

We build mountain ranges of math problems. We skip count up simple concepts of +1 or arduous days of regrouping and equivalent fractions.

Then we roll down hills of laughter, delight of whales, and wonder. The air resistance slows us down so we don't roll too quickly. At the bottom, we relax into the wonder of sky, stars, planets, and our sun as we ride our spaceship "Earth."

We have journeyed far and wide. The third grade looms there, just on the other side of summer. On our adventure, we have learned more than a book could hold. We have learned we all are special with our own set of skills. Those who we started with have all grown from seven to eight. The front teeth are now humongous. The bangs are grown out. The smiles and twinkling eyes are slightly dimmed by concerns over the next adventure, but off my kids skip anyway. And they really are my kids, mine forever. I am confident they are ready.

I paddle my boat slowly, reflectively thinking of all the lessons my seven- and eight-year-old teachers taught me, back to the opposite shore to prepare for my new journey.

About the Author

"The journey of a thousand miles begins with a single step." **Lao Tzu**
Lee-Ann Meredith is a second grade teacher, author, Grade Level Chairperson and education advocate who has spent the duration of her time in public education at John B. Murphy Elementary School in inner city Chicago. Often characterized as funny, dynamic, and an independent innovator, Lee-Ann cites her idol as Ms. Frizzle from *The Magic School Bus*. Fluent in a wide range in instructional strategies for the elementary level, Lee-Ann is dedicated to being an advocate for children everywhere by implementing 'cutting edge' strategies to increase student achievement. Some of the issues that she spearhead included: promoting literacy throughout the building, leading community meetings to advocate for full day kindergarten for all students and helping implement the Responsive Classroom strategies throughout the school. In addition to working closely with the curriculum, she also had the honor to supervise (and mentor into teaching positions) numerous student teachers and practicum students from various post-secondary institutions around the Chicago area such as: Erikson Institute, National Louis, DePaul. Northeastern Illinois, Roosevelt, and North Park Universities.

Born in Gary, Indiana, Lee-Ann was the oldest of six children, Lee-Ann found herself practicing her teacher skills from an early age and with a captive audience. In 1983 Lee-Ann married her husband, Mark, a kind, gentle, smart man who helped her raise two children, Alec and Elena . When their kids were thirteen and eleven years old, Mark was diagnosed with colorectal cancer and unfortunately died three years later.

Marred by her husband's untimely death due to colon cancer, Lee-Ann wrote the memoir, <u>Angels in My Classroom: How Second Graders Saved My Life</u>, to document how her students brought her joy in her utmost time of need. Currently Lee-Ann uses her time to be a freelance writer on issues occurring in education, traveling to be with her grandchildren, being a Usui Reiki Master and promoting her book. For speaking engagements, calendars of dates and ways to book her for a visit to your school, visit her at http://www.leeannmeredith.com.   **Photo Credit: Chad Leverenz.**

CPSIA information can be obtained
at www.ICGtesting.com
Printed in the USA
LVHW052312070722
722996LV00001B/47